Copyright © 2011 by Behaviordilia,

All rights reserved.

No part of this book may be reproduced in any form or by any electronic or mechanical means including information storage and retrieval systems, without permission in writing from the author. The only exception is by a reviewer, who may quote short excerpts in a review.

Richard W. Malott
Websites: www.DickMalott.com, www.behaviordilia.com

Behaviordilia
8971 W. KL Avenue
Kalamazoo MI 49009
USA

(269) 372-1268

New Edition: 2011
First Printing: 1971

ISBN 0-914-47408-1

BE CONSISTENT

"CONSISTENT! YOU JUST SAID THE MAGIC WORD, AND WON A WARM, SINCERE, HANDSHAKE!"

"THE COROLLARY TO NOTHING IN MODERATION IS"

"UNFORTUNATELY, THESE RULES SOUND LIKE THE MINDLESS TRUISMS FROM WHICH WE SPEND MOST OF OUR LIVES TRYING TO FREE OURSELVES. THEY'RE HARD TO APPRECIATE UNTIL YOU'VE HAD SOME FIRST-HAND EXPERIENCE AT CONTINGENCY MANAGEMENT."

COVERT BEHAVER

A FEW MONTHS LATER

"I'LL HAVE TO HAND IT TO YOU CAPTAIN CON. MAN. YOU SURE SAVED MY CAREER!"

"AW, SHUCKS, IT WARN'T NOTHIN'. YOU DID ALL THE WORK."

"BUT.... SIGH... HOW'D YOU DO IT CON. MAN? SURELY THIS CASE HISTORY ILLUSTRATES SOME OF THE UNDERLYING PRINCIPLES OF.... SIGH.... CONTINGENCY MANAGEMENT."

YES MARSHA, THIS CASE, CASE NUMBER 2679 IN THE ANNALS OF THE F.B.I.* ILLUSTRATES THE BASIC PHASES OF CONTINGENCY MANAGEMENT: SPECIFICATION, OBSERVATION, AND CONSEQUATION. FIRST, WE **SPECIFY** THREE THINGS:

THE <u>DESIRED BEHAVIOR</u> — TURNING IN A CHAPTER.

THE <u>CONSEQUENCE</u> — LOSS OF A HUNDRED DOLLAR CHECK, AND

THE <u>CONTINGENCY</u> — EMITTING THE DESIRED BEHAVIOR EACH MONTH AVOIDED THE AVERSIVE CONSEQUENCE. WHENEVER THE DESIRED BEHAVIOR FAILED TO OCCUR, THE AVERSIVE CONSEQUENCE RESULTED.

I MAY HAVE A PH.D., BUT WHAT DO YOU MEAN BY "CONTINGENCY"?

A <u>CONTINGENCY</u> IS A RELATION BETWEEN TWO EVENTS. IF ONE EVENT OCCURS, THEN THE OTHER EVENT FOLLOWS. IF YOU TURN A CHAPTER IN ON TIME, YOU KEEP THE HUNDRED DOLLARS. IF YOU ARE LATE, YOU LOSE THE HUNDRED DOLLARS. OUR CONTINGECY IS THE RELATION BETWEEN YOUR BEHAVIOR AND THE CONSEQUENCE.

* FREAKED-OUT BEHAVIORAL INSTRUCTORS

SO, THE FIRST THING WE DO IS SPECIFY THE _____, THE _____, AND THE _____. THEN WE **OBSERVE** WHETHER OR NOT THE BEHAVIOR OCCURS, AND FINALLY WE CONSEQUATE THE BEHAVIOR APPROPRIATELY.

CONSEQUATE?

APPLY THE CONSEQUENCES: KEEP THE HUNDRED DOLLARS OR SEND IT TO THE F.F.A.

AH YES! AND WE MUST **NOT** BE MODERATE OR REASONABLE IN OUR CONSEQUATION BUT MUST CONSEQUATE CONSISTENTLY.

A DIABOLICAL DIALOGUE (OR TRIALOGUE)

Question: This avoidance contingency is all very good, but it seems so negative. Couldn't you use some sort of positive contingency?

Answer: Yes, in fact it's called a POSITIVE REINFORCEMENT CONTINGENCY. Instead of taking away $100 when John failed to turn in a chapter on time, Capt. Con. Man. could have given him $100 each time he did turn in a chapter on time.

Q: So why didn't he use the positive reinforcement contingency?

A: You must be kidding. That would have cost Capt. Con. Man. $600 out of his own meager salary, and you can be sure that no one cons Con. Man.

Q: Would the positive rein-------- con-------- have worked if Capt. Con. Man. had been generous enough to try it?

A: My guess is that since the avoid---- con-------- worked the pos----- re---------- co--------- would also work. I don't know of any experiments on this problem, but my casual observation has been that failing to earn $100 will have about the same effect as losing $100.

Q: Now wait a minute. If this is a po----- r---------- c---------, how can he fail to earn his $100 each time he turns in a chapter. Won't he get $100 each time he turns in a chapter?

A: I'm afraid I slipped that one over on you. If you'll read a few paragraphs back, you'll see that I said John had to turn his chapters in on time. There was a deadline even with the p------ r---------- c---------.

Q: Were the deadlines necessary? It seems like the $100 positive reinforcement would have been enough to keep John writing those chapters.

A: The deadlines might not have been needed, but it's hard to say. That really is an empirical question.

Q: What do you mean, "empirical question?"

A: An empirical question can be answered best by actually looking at the situation you're wondering about to see what's happening. Simply sitting in our armchairs and speculating is not good enough.

Q: Wowie! I get it. Be a spectator, not a speculator.

A: An empirical solution to your question means that John would have to work on a pos---------- r---------- c---------- without a deadline and we would see if he got his dissertation written.

Q: It seems to me that John would work better without deadlines. At least, I've heard a lot of people say they do.

A: I've heard people say the same thing. These are usually people who've not had much experience working with deadlines. What they mean is that working with deadlines is sometimes aversive, and sometimes they end up working harder than they would like. But in most cases, they'll find that without any deadlines, they'll not work as hard as they'd like.

Q: Why is that?

A: In John's case, part of it'll depend on what he's going to do with that $100. If he needs the $100 each month to keep up the payments on his new Volkswagen with the power steering, power brakes, electric windows, built-in tape deck with the 1000 watt amp (each channel) and the 30-inch woofers, simulated zebra skin upholstery, mud flaps, fuzzy dice hung from the rearview mirror, genuine plastic dashboard statue of Captain Contingency Management, chrome plated fender dent, and a "BETTER LIVING THROUGH BEHAVIORISM" bumper sticker, then we don't need to worry about imposing deadlines. The bank will do it for us.

Q: Yeah, but the bank has set up a(n)
   a. avoidance contingency
       or
   b. positive reinforcement contingency
of its own.

A: Correct, John writes the chapter, gets the $100, and gives it to the bank. He avoids losing the Volkswagen. I suspect that some sort of deadlines are usually present in situations where people are productive; however, sometimes they may not be very obvious. In fact, I've known people who were very productive in some areas and not so productive in similar areas. If you looked closely, you'd see the presence or absence of the deadline contingency. Many people who do scientific research get research grants to help support their efforts. To get a grant you have to write an elaborate proposal which has to be sent to the granting agency by a certain deadline. If the deadline is missed, you have to wait several months for the next one. As a result of this deadline, most scientists are able to find the time to get their grant proposals written. After an experiment is completed, you may report the results at a professional meeting. This means you must have your results analyzed and your talk prepared by the time of the meeting; another deadline and again most scientists have little difficulty finding the time to do this. Finally, scientists should write up reports of their successful experiments and publish them in scientific journals. There are no deadlines for submitting articles to journals, and as a result many scientists have difficulty getting around to writing up their journal articles.

Q: If the journals had deadlines, then more scientists would get their research written up?
A: Probably a deadline like this would do the trick: All articles to be published within the next two years must be submitted by January 1.

Q: That's a(n)
  a. avoidance contingency
    or
  b. positive reinforcement contingency.
A: The publication of the article is a positive reinforcer, and it will occur if the desired behavior occurs.

Q: So of course it's a(n)
  a. avoidance contingency
    or
  b. positive reinforcement contingency.

Q: Why don't publishers of journals use a contingency management procedure like that?
A: For one thing, the resulting increase in the number of articles they would receive would be a punisher instead of a reinforcer. In spite of the fact that many scientists do not produce as many articles as they should, the journals still receive many more articles than they can publish.

Q: Would this sort of contingency management procedure be useful for book publishers?
A: Yes, that's a different problem. There are hundreds of fine, intelligent, honorable, industrious men who have agreed with publishers to write books for them and have copped out. They may even write a chapter or two, but they never get around to the next one. They plan to next week, but something else always comes up. If the publishers could use a positive reinforcement contingency with a set of deadlines, most of those books would probably be written by now.

Q: If these contingency management procedures are so good, why don't the book publishers use them?
A: There are several reasons. First, they don't understand contingency management as well as you or I do. Not only don't they understand the solution, they don't even understand the problem.

Q: Well, supose some smart guy like you explained the problem and solution to them. Would the book publishers use contingency management then?
A: They still may not. They might correctly anticipate too much static from their authors. Many people (including would-be authors) continue to believe in the myth that they will be most productive when there are no deadlines. They are also morally offended to think that they need artificial rewards or reinforcers such as $$$ to get them to write their books. They believe that anyone who can't get a book written for sheer love of writing it is a lowly form of humanity.

Q: And many of them will not get their books written themselves?
A: Right.

Suddenly, distant but eerie laughter pierces the tranquility of our gentle dialogue. The laughter grows nearer and then a blinding flash of light, more powerful than the mighty strobes of Filmores East and West combined, floods the scene with a diabolic luminescence. On recovering the use of our visual faculty (eyes), we see a nattily dressed man in what appears to be the simulation of a college professor's suit, i. e., tweed coat with leather elbow patches, pipe, and wrinkled trousers (which have obviously been worn for the last semester). But there is a visual dissonance: in descending order, his hat is pulled down too snugly over his head, he werars ear muffs (though it is July), he wears shades (though it is night time), his little black goatee is unfashionably pointed, the seat of his pants is much too baggy, and his shoes appear to have no toes in them. Who or what is this abberated apparition? We know, don't we?

?????: Well, well, Answer, you certainly have been brainwashing young Question here. Any author worth his salt can write books without your contingency management crutch. The idea of using money as a reward or reinforcer for the authors is nothing more than bribery, or my mother's name's not Rosemary.

A: Just a moment, Mr. ?????, you're using one of the most despicable techniques known to argumentation.

Curses, thinks Mr. ?????, Answer's penetrating intellect and honesty will make a shambles of my admittedly shabby argument.

A (continues): You're forcing negative words on us, like "brainwashing," "crutch," and "bribery," even though they don't fit. You hope to win this diabolic dialogue by prejudicing young Question here against contingency management without a careful, clear, and honest analysis of the procedures we advocate.

?????: Ugh.

A: You say I'm "brainwashing" young Question here. I've heard that one before. To the best of my humble ability, I tell it like it is. Whenever people start picking up on what I'm laying down, some mindmuddler like you screams "Brainwashing!" I'm using honest means of persuasion; "brainwashing" implies dishonest means. Whenever someone does a convincing job of presenting something you don't like, you use a negative word like "brainwashing." In fact, what you're trying to do is really "brainwashing."

?????: Oh, yeah. You don't present both sides of the story, and that's brainwashing.

A: Young Question here already knows most of

your side of the story; it's part of the nonsense our culture programs into us at an early and defenseless age. But why do you think we let a slob like you in here? The only reason we tolerate you is so that you can present arguments that Question here might not have thought of.

?????: Gasp!

A: And I must say, you're disappointingly inarticulate. You get your jollies by arguing against some young dude who's just been turned on to contingency management. You win an argument with a student who isn't on to your tricks, and you act as if you've wiped out the whole technology of contingency management. But you've met your match this time, ?????.

?????: (I'm losing ground fast.....) Be serious, Answer, you'll have to admit that contingency management is nothing more than a crutch for the weak.

Q: Gee, Mr. Answer Man. I'm afraid he's got you this time.

A: Be patient, my young friend; I think we can handle this one, too. But notice that old ????? can't talk without slyly slipping in more negative words like "weak." What I'm saying is that we can all function better with proper contingency management.

?????: BETTER LIVING THROUGH BEHAVIORISM! Bah, humbug!

A: If I were a nutritionist, I might suggest an improved diet which would help us function better. Even you wouldn't argue that an improved diet is a mere crutch for the weak. In the same way, an improved diet of the contingencies of reinforcement is not a crutch for the psychologically weak. Psychology, the science of behavior, tells us why we do what we do; the technology of contingency management tells us how to arrange our environment so that we will do what we want to do.

Q: Golly Ned, Mr. Answer Man, that was brilliant.

?????: (We'll see if Mr. Answer Man can parry my third and final thrust.) You may not be brainwashing young Question here, and con------------man----------------- may not be a crutch, but any way you look at it, using money as a reward or rein------------------ to get authors to write their books smacks of bribery.

A: There you go again with your insidious word game. Young Question here, you have to be careful with men who use emotional words as a substitute for rational argument. They try to confuse the issue. Bribery may make use of rewards or re-------------------- or threats to influence people to do things which they should not do, to do things which are wrong. Suppose unscrupulous publishers used re-------- to get the authors to write books full of lies, statements which both the publishers and the authors knew were false; that would be bribery. The honorable use of contingency management may involve a similar arrangement of contingencies and consequences, but the desired behavior is not wrong; it is right. It is not wrong for authors to write books of truth. The difference between the honorable and dishonorable use of contingency management is in the behavior specified, not the contingencies or consequences.

Q: The jig's up for you, Mr. ?????. Speaking for myself and the rest of the youth in this great nation of ours, you can just go to Hell.

?????: (Curses, zapped again.) There's no place I'd rather be, you presumptuous waif, you. And as for you, my arch foe, you've won this round; but when we meet again the tables may be turned.

Gradually proximal but insipid sobbing fades into tranquility. There is a faint puff of smoke, the lingering smell of burnt gunpowder (a cheap theatrical trick), and the forces of evil are no more.

Perhaps we've milked the case of Johnathan Procrastinator for as much as we should. When you can correctly answer all of the following questions, you're cool.

WHAT KIND OF MAN READS CONTINGENCY MANAGEMENT IN EDUCATION AND OTHER EQUALLY EXCITING PLACES, OR, I'VE GOT BLISTERS ON MY SOUL AND OTHER EQUALLY EXCITING PLACES?

A MAN WHO, IN SPITE OF A HIGHLY REINFORCING SEX LIFE, FINDS TIME TO ACTIVELY PURSUE HIS ACADEMIC OR PROFESSIONAL CAREER. HE MAY BE A HIGH SCHOOL SENIOR, A COLLEGE FRESHMAN, A GRADUATE STUDENT, OR A PROFESSIONAL WITH A PH.D., BUT HE KNOWS WHERE HIS REINFORCERS LAY AND LETS NO FALSE PRETENSES INTERFERE WITH THEIR ATTAINMENT.

This chapter was very loosely based on Nurnberger, J. I. and Zimmerman, J. Applied Analysis of Human Behavior: An Alternative to Conventional Motivation Inferences and Unconscious Determination in Therapeutic Programming. <u>Behavior Therapy</u>, 1970, 1, 59—69.

RECAP

A reinforcing stimulus must increase the future probability of a response, or it is not a reinforcer. You might think that this is a trivial distinction; however, it's very important in behavior analysis. It is too easy to say that an event is reinforcing, but without empirical data we can only speak of that event's appeal to us.

1. A reinforcing stimulus is roughly the same as a reward; however, it is not exactly the same. A reward refers to doing something for, or giving something to someone as an expression of gratitude. A reward implies no effect on future behavior.

Too often people try to change behavior by using consequences that they think are reinforcing or punishing. When the behavior fails to change, they claim that the procedure is at fault........perhaps all that was needed was a more effective consequence. There is no such thing as a reinforcer that doesn't work, because by definition a reinforcer increases the future probability of a response it follows. If an event does not do this, it is not a reinforcer.

2. Behavior is controlled by its consequences; it is controlled best by those consequences that immediately follow the behavior. Most students avoid studying until one or two nights before the test, when it may be more effective to study every night. The reason students do not study every night is that there is no immediate consequence for not studying. The night before the test, the consequence for not studying is poor test performance, which is relatively immediate after an all-nighter.

3. The rules "Nothing in Moderation" and "Be Consistent" are important for the same reasons that immediate consequences are important. Behavior is best controlled by those consequences that are applied consistently. If you only did poorly on 1/3 of the tests you didn't study for, you probably wouldn't study for tests. If you consistently flunked tests after not studying, you would probably study for more tests.

4. Contingency Management requires the specification of behaviors, consequences, and contingencies. We have already seen that behavior is best controlled by immediate, consistent consequences. If you want to teach your dog to do something, you must first know what you want him to do, what you will use as a consequence, and when to apply that consequence (contingency). If you don't know all three of these, you can't be consistent.

5. A contingency is similar to a cause-effect relation between two events. In psychology, a contingency means: if a behavior occurs, then a consequence will follow. The type of consequence that follows determines the type of contingency in use.

To answer an empirical question is to OBSERVE what is happening — you might say that "seeing is believing."

6. Behavioral psychology as a science has evolved into the empirical study of behavior. This means that the psychologist looks at situations and behavior, manipulates various aspects of those situations, and observes any resultant changes in behavior.

OBJECTIVES

1. A reinforcing stimulus is roughly the same as a(n) _____.
   a) result
   b) strengthened response
   c) reward
   d) specified behavior
   e) additional company of soldiers

2. The probability of future occurrences of a response is INCREASED when that response is followed by a(n) _____.
   a) reinforcer
   b) punisher
   c) avoidance contingency
   d) future response
   e) consequence

3. The first rule of contingency management is _____.
   a) nothing in excess
   b) nothing in moderation
   c) nothing at all
   d) S.O.C.
   e) there is no such thing as contingency management

4. In contingency management it is important to apply the contingencies _____.
   a) in moderation
   b) at least occasionally
   c) intermittently
   d) consistently
   e) there is no SET rule about the application of the contingencies.

5. The three basic phases of contingency management are _____, _____, and _____. (choose three)
   a) behavior
   b) observation
   c) consequation
   d) contingency application
   e) S.O.O.
   f) moderation
   g) consistent application
   h) specification

6. If one event occurs, then another event will follow. This relationship between a behavior and its consequence is known as a(n) _____.
   a) observation
   b) relevant relation
   c) expectation
   d) fact
   e) contingency

7. The first step of contingency management is to _____ the behavior, consequence and the contingincies.
   a) specify
   b) observe
   c) consequate
   d) structure
   e) control
   f) objectify

8. The second step of contingency management is to _____ whether or not the behavior occurs.
   a) specify
   b) observe
   c) consequate
   d) control
   e) structure
   f) objectify

9. The third step of contingency management is to _____ the behavior appropriately.
   a) specify
   b) observe
   c) consequate
   d) control
   e) structure
   f) objectify

10. A(n) _____ approach to a question means to look at the situation and see what's happening.
    a) parsimonious
    b) observical
    c) deterministic
    d) empirical
    e) mentalistic

11. If a question is an empirical question, it means that it can only be answered by _____.
    a) observation
    b) speculation
    c) ingenuity
    d) creative thought
    e) "Mom"

12. The difference between "brainwashing" and other more acceptable means of persuasion is that brainwashing implies _____.
    a) force
    b) dishonesty
    c) negative reinforcement
    d) mystery
    e) hypnosis

13. _____ tells us why we do what we do.
    a) Psychology (science of behavior)
    b) Contingency management
    c) S.O.C.
    d) The environment
    e) Our conscience

14. _____ tells us how to arrange our environment so that we will do what we want to.
    a) Psychology (science of behavior)
    b) Contingency management
    c) S.O.C.
    d) Environmental Management
    e) Education

15. The difference between bribery and other more acceptable means of persuasion is that in bribery the desired behavior is _____ .
    a) wrong
    b) painful
    c) dirty
    d) desirable
    e) unavoidable

16. The difference between honorable and dishonorable use of contingency management is the _____ , not the _____ .
    (Choose two answers in the correct order.)
    a) contingencies
    b) environment
    c) behavior specified
    d) intent
    e) corruption

ANSWERS

1. c; 2. a; 3. b; 4. d; 5. b, c, h (any order); 6. e; 7. a; 8. b; 9. c; 10. d; 11. a; 12. b; 13. a; 14. b; 15. a; 16. c, a, (in that order).

INTRODUCTION

O. K., the goal of this book is to turn you on to the principles of behavior and YOU. So now all we have to do is write the book.

Quit screwing around and write the book.

I'm not screwing around; I'm thinking. And besides, I'm not really into writing today. I'll get started on it tomorrow.

TOMORROW: I wish I had time to get started writing today; I'm really up for it, but I've got to give two lectures, counsel students, and go to the faculty meeting.

TOMORROW'S TOMORROW: Before I get started, maybe I should change the typewriter ribbon. And I've got only 50 sheets of paper; I'd better get some more. It sure would be a bummer to run out of paper when I'm right in the middle of my work.

And now.......oh, phooey, here comes a student for counseling. I'll have to talk to him for awhile before I can start on my writing.

If another student comes in, I'll just tell him I'm busy. And now......oh, tarnation, here comes the chairman of our department, I can't tell him I'm too busy.

Gee whiz, it's time to go home to supper, and I still haven't gotten any writing done.

AND STILL ANOTHER DAY: The only thing to do is to put up a "Do Not Disturb" sign and lock my office door.

Now I'll get out my typewriter and........."Hey, can't you read? That sign says 'Do Not Disturb'."

"I just wanted to know when you'd be available to talk."

Oh, crime-in-itely. "You've already interrupted me, so come in and let's get it over with."

That was a very disturbing talk, and now I don't feel at all like writing. Think I'd better wait until tomorrow.

(Jimmy Hendrix sings in the background, "Think I'd better wait 'til tomorrow.")

AND THAT TOMORROW: Clearly there's too much going on at my office for me to get any writing done, so maybe I'd better stay at home this morning. But I don't have my typewriter here. I'll just go in to school for a couple 'a seconds, get my typewriter, and come on back home.

Now that I'm at school, I might as well look thru this morning's mail and see if there's anything important.

Oh, thunder. I have to give a lecture in 45 minutes, so I might as well bag writing for today.

THE NEXT DAY: It sure is quiet at home. Now I'm really going to get some writing done.

I wonder what's happening at school. I'll drop in for a while to check out the scene.

O. K., man, admit it. You're a lazy slob and you're never going to get that book written.

I may be a slob, and I may not get that book written, but I'm not lazy. I put in as much time working as anyone else does.

Then, you hard-working son-of-a-gun, you, the truth must be that you don't really want to write that book.

No, I really want to write the book. Writing the book is the most important thing I can do.

If it's so important, why don't you write it?

Well, there're all these little things that keep cropping up. They have to be attended to. As long as I can put off writing until tomorrow, I end up doing all of these little piddling things.

So why weren't you able to write when you stayed home? The first thing you did was cop out on some hokey pretext and go back to school.

I hate to admit it, but I guess I really enjoy talking to my colleagues and counseling students. Those kinds of activities are very reinforcing.*

Then give up on your writing and go on and spend the rest of your life talking to students and colleagues.

But I REALLY do want to write that book. I wish these other people weren't so readily available to me. Then I might get my book written and still have time to do all that talking I find so reinforcing.

---

*A "REINFORCER" is roughly the same thing as a reward. If you do something that produces a reinforcer, then you will probably do that again in the future. If talking to people is reinforcing, then you will probably do the sorts of things which bring you into contact with people and result in talking with them.

HERE'S WHERE WE'RE AT

THIS IS OUR MESSAGE

THIS WE BELIEVE

First, we are BEHAVIORISTS: we believe that the problems of psychology can be best expressed in terms of behavior. What man thinks, sees, feels, wants, and knows — what man is — can be most efficiently studied in terms of what man does, how he behaves.

Second, we are DETERMINISTS: we believe there are reasons for man's behavior. Man's behavior is caused.

Third, we are ENVIRONMENTALISTS: we believe that the causes of man's behavior are to be found in his environment.

Fourth, we are LEARNING THEORISTS: we believe that the environment causes man to be what he is by teaching him to behave as he does.

Fifth, we are REINFORCEMENT THEORISTS: we believe that the results of our behavior determine whether we will behave that way in the future. The results reinforce the behavior.

Sixth, we are PERFECTIONISTS: we believe that man can approximate perfection thru the arrangement of his environment so that behavior he considers desirable is reinforced.

and

Seventh, we are REALISTS: we believe that the optimal arrangement of man's environment is a very difficult task.

This may not make too much sense to you now. Don't worry, it should be considerably clearer by the time you are done.

or

You may understand it, disagree vehemently, and be completely turned off. Stay with us for awhile.

We're trying to tell you where our head is at, in front. That may not be the most effective way of convincing you of the reasonableness of a set of unpopular beliefs. But it is the most honest way. We're not trying to brainwash. But we are trying to persuade.

MAN'S BIGGEST PROBLEM IS THAT
HIS BEHAVIOR IS MORE EASILY
INFLUENCED BY
SMALL, BUT IMMEDIATE
REINFORCERS
THAN IT IS BY
LARGE, BUT DISTANT REINFORCERS.

The Original Sin:

That apple tastes good,
like sin should,
but it's not really that great,
but it's right NOW,
(and even Adam & Eve were part of
the NOW GENERATION),
and eternity in paradise
is a long, long way off.

Damned, I wish I could quit smoking.

So, why don't you?

    I don't know. I've tried several times; but I always go right back to the weed. I just don't have enough will power.

    If you REALLY wanted to quit smoking, you could.

    That's not true. I'd pay a lot of money to quit smoking. I know I'm probably going to die of lung cancer. I really want to quit smoking, but I can't. And the funny thing is, I don't really enjoy smoking all that much.

What is the wicked behavior?
    The response of inhaling thru the cigarette.

What is the evil reinforcer?
    The nicotine-filled smoke invading your lungs.

What is paradise lost?
    The wonderful but distant reinforcer of a long and healthy life.

So there you are,
    the inhaling response is more easily influenced by the small, crummy, but immediate reinforcer of nicotine in the lungs
    than it is by the large, beautiful, but distant reinforcer of a long and healthy life.

See the pretty diagram. It says the same thing.

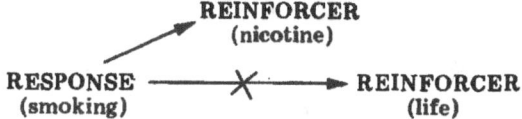

It happens to the best of us.

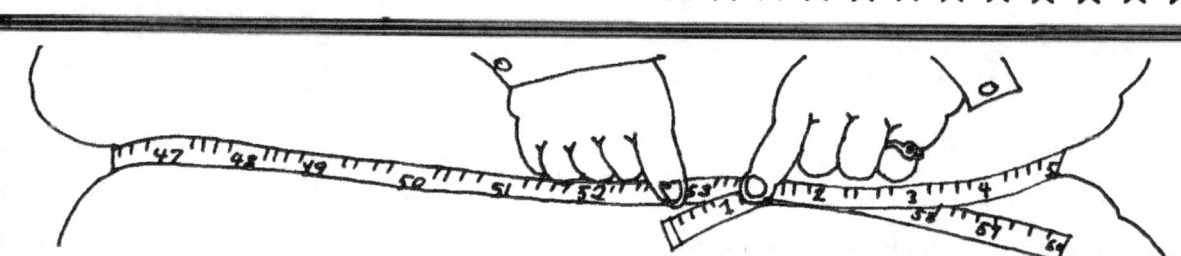

Damned, I wish I could stop eating so much.

So, why don't you?

    I don't know. I've tried several times; but everytime I go right back to gluttony. I just don't have enough will power.

    If you really wanted to diet, you would.

    That's not true. I'd pay a lot of money to lose a few pounds. I know I'm probably going to die of a coronary because I'm overweight. I really want to quit overeating, but I can't. And the funny thing is, I don't really enjoy the extra food all that much.

The undesirable behavior;
    The response of overeating.

The bad reinforcer?
    The excess food invading your body.

The good reinforcer?
    The distant but valuable long and healthy life.

So there,
    The overeating response is more easily influenced by the small, disgusting, but immediate reinforcer of food in the gut
    than it is by the large, fantastic, but distant reinforcer of a long and healthy life.

See.

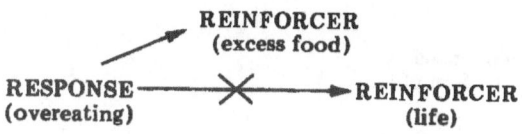

The distant but more valuable reinforcer loses again.

Jog a mile every day.
Strengthen that heart muscle.
You'll live longer.

I wish I could keep up with my exercises.

So?

I've tried, several times, to exercise on a regular basis; but I always start slacking off and then quit. No will power.

You don't really want to.

No, I'd pay top dollar if I could hang in there. I'll die young because of a flabby heart. I really want to be a jogging jock. It's funny. I have plenty of time to do my exercises, but I don't do 'em.

Wait a minute. This doesn't quite fit into our old familiar pattern. Instead of trying to get rid of undesirable behavior, we're trying to GET some desirable behavior--we're trying to get a little jogging behavior on the road.

So what's the problem?

Jogging is hard work. Hard work usually is not too reinforcing. In fact, it may be the opposite of reinforcing. It's punishing. If you do something that is punished, then you'll be less likely to try that one again in the future.

A PUNISHER decreases the probability of responses which produce it.

A REINFORCER increases the probability of responses which produce it.

Good behavior?
The response of jogging a mile.

Punisher?
The hard work and exhaustion associated with jogging.

Reinforcer?
Long life.

So,
the jogging response is more easily influenced by the small, invigorating, but immediate punisher, hard work,
than it is by the large, priceless, but distant reinforcer of long life.

If you don't think life is priceless, ask yourself, "If I knew I would normally live to the age of 70 years, how much money would I have to be paid, RIGHT NOW, to agree to be put painlessly to death at the age of 65?" How much is the last five years of your life worth right now?

Really think about it.

Yet you are making all sorts of responses that decrease the expected length of your life. And you don't spend a few minutes every day making those responses that increase the expected length of your life. And the reinforcers that maintain those harmful responses are worth only a fraction of the reinforcer of a longer and healthier life.

The diagram:

RESPONSE (jogging) → PUNISHER (work)
RESPONSE (jogging) → POSITIVE REINFORCER (life)

And what happens when the same response produces both an immediate but trivial punisher and a distant but huge reinforcer? We know, don't we? Immediacy wins out every time. The punisher wins. The response stops occurring.

A clarification: when we say "punisher," we don't necessarily mean that there is someone doing the punishing. If you're a little clumsy when hammering a nail, you may hit your thumb. The ensuing pain is a "punisher." You will be less likely to hammer your thumb in the future. The probability of the thumb-hammering response has decreased.

I wish I could keep up with my homework. I've got so much reading to do for this course, it's really a drag.

Everytime I sit down to read, someone invites me to go down to the Knollwood Tavern for a quick beer. Or else I get into a heavy conversation with my room-mates about sex, religion, or politics (i. e., whether cops should beat up college kids). And besides, the book is boring as hell and hard to read.

That's cool man. Books ain't where it's at. Be free. Do your own thing.

No, I really want to be a good student. I know I'll probably flunk the midterm, but goofing off is so much more fun than studying, and that exam is so far away. Well, I'll probably get a bad grade in the course because I spend all my time at the Knollwood. The funny thing is, I don't really like beer; it makes me...............ah....................
        too much.
a. belch
b. ?????

And the plot gets still thicker: we've got immediate punishers AND immediate reinforcers and even competing responses.

Good behavior?
    Studying.

Punisher?
    Hard work, confusion, boredom.

Bad competing behavior?
    Goofing off.

Bad reinforcer?
    Excessive socializing with the gang.

Good reinforcer?
    Learning a lot and getting a good grade.

The studying response is more easily influenced by the small, but immediate punisher, hard work; the goofing-off response is more easily influenced by the small, but immediate reinforcer of excessive socializing than by the large, but distant reinforcers of valuable knowledge and a good grade.

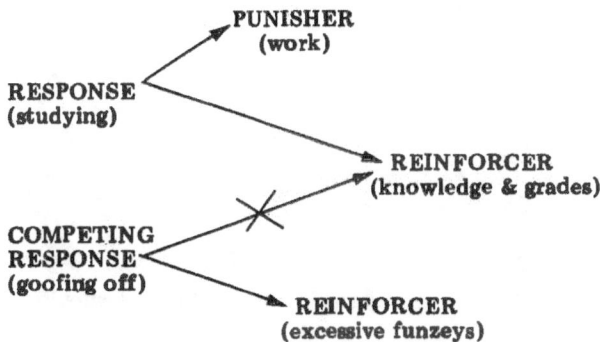

Even if there weren't fellow students around to reinforce goofing off, the hard work that results from studying might be enough of a punisher to pretty much wipe it out. But when you add an incompatible response that competes with studying, and when you reinforce that incompatible goofing-off response with a little of that sweet old good times, then watch out. The delicate, fragile response known as studying has definitely had it. There goes knowledge, good grades, and the good life, right out the dormitory window.

RATED GP

(PARENTAL GUIDANCE SUGGESTED)

Oh, Oh, Oh. . . . . .

Uhmmmm. . . . .

Ooooohhh. . . . .

Uhm. . . . .

Wait, do you have one of those things?

No, aren't you taking the ah...?

No. Maybe we'd better not then.

Ok, we won't.

Ooooohh.

Uhm..

Oh.

Um.

Oh, oh, ohhh.

. . . .

That was pretty risky. I don't think we should have.

Probably not.

```
                    REINFORCER
                 (tactual stimulation)
                   ↗
RESPONSE   ─────────→   PUNISHER
(Oh, you know)       (making it a threesome)
```

The response is more easily influenced by the smaller but immediate reinforcer than by the large but distant punisher.

Notice that this is the first example where the consequence in the distance was a punisher. We could just as easily have said "keeping it a twosome is a reinforcer." And in the previous examples we could have said ignorance, poor grades, and a short, unhealthy life were punishers. It doesn't seem to matter how you say it; the distant consequence still takes it in the ear.

We've been looking at these everyday dilemmas in an attempt to convince you that behavior is more easily influenced by immediate, though unimportant, consequences than it is by distant, though very significant, consequences.

Since we've introduced the notion of "punishers", we can't just talk about immediate and distant reinforcers. We must also talk about immediate and distant punishers. We'll use the term "consequence" to refer to the results of behavior when we don't want to specify whether those results are reinforcing or punishing.

Before we go any further, let's look at the reasons for the ineffectiveness of distant reinforcers and punishers. The mere fact that a consequence is distant may not be the only reason for its weakness.

Stop what you're doing right now. Go to the nearest blackboard and write, "BEHAVIOR IS A RESULT OF ITS CONSEQUENCES," 1000 times, and I'll give you $10,000 twenty years from now.

If you believed me, you'd do it, even though the reinforcer is a long way off.

If you KNOW that a little responding right now will definitely produce a big reinforcer in the future, you'll do it.

What about this?
If you don't take one more drag on that fag, you'll live to be 100. But if you take so much as a single puff, you die at the age of 65.

You'll never touch that dreaded weed again.

If that consequence is definite, if it is certain, then it can have a powerful effect on your behavior.
If it is not certain, if it is only a possibility, then it has very little effect.

Everytime you get in your automobile, you increase the odds that you'll die young. Speed, and you increase the odds even further. Have a couple of drinks, and you increase the odds still further.
But you'll PROBABLY get by anyway.
But there's carnage on all our highways.

When we talk about being killed in a car accident, we're talking about RIGHT NOW. We're not talking about the distant future.

An important consequence doesn't have to be distant to be ineffective.
If it is immediate but uncertain, it may also be ineffective.

When people go scuba diving or sky diving, they greatly increase the chances of immediate death.

But since they will probably live to tell about it, they keep diving.
Not many people jumb out of a plan without a parachute, however, because death is just TOO probable.

In some college courses, a student caught cheating on an hour exam receives an "F" in the course, an immediate punisher.
But there is SOME CHANCE that he will get by undetected, and so occasionally a student takes that chance.
No student cheats when detection seems highly probable.

THE LESS PROBABLE A CONSEQUENCE, THE LESS EFFECTIVE THE CONSEQUENCE.

What about studying for that exam? If I don't study, I'll fail; that's certain. A very definite punisher.
But I can goof off for just five more minutes; that probably won't hurt.
The problem is I can always put off studying just a little bit longer. The response of goofing off for just five more minutes PROBABLY won't have any effect on my grade. After all, how much can I learn in just five minutes? Those five minute periods add up, and all of a sudden I only have time to read about a quarter of my assignment. My God, how time flies. And I blow the exam.
But the probability is very low that any particular five minutes of goofing off is going to hurt you.

THE LESS PROBABLE THE CONSEQUENCE, THE LESS EFFECTIVE THE CONSEQUENCE.

Does that mean that the remoteness of the consequence doesn't matter?

Does that mean that distant consequences are just as effective as immediate consequences?

No. Suppose I said, "Push button No. 1 and you get $5 now; push button No. 2 and you get $5 ten years from now." We know which button you'd push, don't we? I could give you $6 for pushing button No. 2, and you'd still go for No. 1.

This truth is still eternal:

THE MORE DISTANT THE CONSEQUENCE, THE LESS EFFECTIVE THE CONSEQUENCE.

The reason life is so difficult is that these two truths are frequently combined. The important consequences are often both distant and uncertain.

But let's keep right on truckin'. We want you to understand we're not just talkin' 'bout all them other guys—we're talkin' 'bout you.

When was the last time you wrote a letter home?

The folks back home really want to hear from you. And you really do want to write them a letter. But almost anything you can imagine is more reinforcing than writing that letter. To put it another way, almost every other thing you might do is less punishing than writing that letter. Even reading this stuff beats writing the letter.

> Dear Son/Daughter,
> (select one)
>
> You've been at college for almost a month, and we haven't heard a word from you. Is everything all right? Everything is o. k. here, except we miss you.
>
> Love,
>
> Mom and/or Dad

Wow. I've really been a heel. I'll write 'em the first thing tomorrow.

Two weeks later the phone rings.

Mom: This is your mother.

Student: Gee, Mom, it's good to hear your voice.

Mom: Is everything all right?

Student: Of course.

Mom: When you didn't answer our letter, we thought maybe you'd o.d'd.

> (A very hip mama)

Student: Everything's o. k.; it really is. And I promise to write tomorrow.

And then it's Thanksgiving or spring vacation, whichever.

Student: Hey, Mom, Dad, I'm home.

Mom: You didn't write.

Student: Gee, Mom, I'm awfully busy.

Mom: If you've been so busy, why did the college send us a letter saying you're on academic probation?

Dad: Been chasing around after those................ that's why.
    a. fraternity boys (select answer
    b. sorority girls   according to your
    c. both a and b   own taste.)

Good behavior?
    Letter writing.

Bad behavior?
    Everything else (including studying).

Immediate reinforcers?
    Having more fun doing everything but writing home.

Immediate punisher?
    The hard work of letter writing. Writing is definitely hard work. Even letter writing is hard.

Distant reinforcer?
    Simply finishing a letter is very reinforcing; and it's not very distant, maybe 20 or 30 minutes from the time you start the letter. But it's still too distant. And then there's the pleasant acknowledgement from your parents when they write a return letter.

Distant and improbable punisher?
    Being bitched at by your parents. Remember:

This is a low probability consequence in the sense that the probability is low that you'll be punished if you don't write today. You can always wait until tomorrow.

So you live at home with your parents and have trouble relating to that letter writing problem. Try this one: remember that really good friend you had who moved away? You both promised to write each other faithfully; but during the last two years you've written only one letter and your friend has written only three. But the thing is you REALLY did want to keep writing. What happened?

If you don't write the letter this morning, you'll PROBABLY still be able to write later on, maybe even this afternoon. But there's no question about it, if you turn that TV set off now, you'll definitely lose those audio-visual reinforcers emanating out of the Ponderosa country. The result is that you clock in hundreds of hours watching TV and zero hours writing letters.

But sometimes the consequences of writing your parents can be quite immediate and then you write the letter:

Dear Mom and Dad:

I finally managed to take time away from my studies to write you this long overdue letter. Everything is real good here at school and I'm learning a lot. By the way, my checking account is getting a little low and I wondered if you could . . . .

While we're on the subject of TV, there is a multi-million dollar industry whose main purpose is to develop a set of immediate but very small, almost miniscule, reinforcers designed to control just one response — your sitting in front of the TV set with the picture and sound on. Imagine that. Millions and millions of dollars are being spent developing a set of tiny but immediate reinforcers with your mind in mind. And those $$$,$$$,$$$ are being spent very effectively; they are controlling millions of man hours out there in television land.

"I don't know why I watch this crap. It's not like I don't have something better to do with my time."

But we know, don't we. Those little worthless reinforcers just keep flowing out of the TV set in a continuous stream.

This really is continuous reinforcement. The reinforcers from TV sometimes get so thick that you have to shovel a path across the living room floor in order to get to the john. Fortunately the consequences of going to the john are usually sufficiently immediate and sufficiently reinforcing that nature is able to compete successfully with the multi-million dollar television industry. Usually. Of course it is just when you were planning to go to the bathroom that television really goes out to deliver the reinforcing goods, i. e., during the commercials.

"Damn it, I meant to hit the head during the commercial, but I got so involved that now I'll have to go during the program instead."

Yes, if you spend over $1000 a second, you can develop a series of sights and sounds that will almost be more reinforcing than nature's call. It seems that novelty is a major factor in determining how reinforcing sight and sound are. The longer you look at the same image on the tube, the less reinforcing it becomes. A sound that's on for a long time will have the same fate. If you wanted to design a television program that had close to zero reinforcing value, what would you do?

"I'd hire a college professor to stand in front of a TV camera and read to us from his lecture notes for 50 minutes."

If you want to have a TV show where someone talks, then you'd better hire an interviewer to interrupt him now and then with silly questions. The next time you watch Johnny Carson, notice that the guests rarely talk for more than 10 seconds without being interrupted. Also notice that they use three different camera angles and no single shot stays on for more than ten seconds.

Gosh, can you think of anything that is more reinforcing than watching Johnny talk to his friends?

"Laugh-In."

Right, if Laugh-In kept the same scene on for more than four or five seconds, they'd think their cameraman was dead. And, of course, there are those new-image-every-second sequences on Sesame Street. Television commercials rarely keep the same picture on your screen for more than three or four seconds. Mason Williams did the ultimate on the old Smothers Brothers show--pictures of famous paintings flashed at the rate of five or ten a second. A classical gas indeed. No one went to the kitchen for a beer during that sequence.

So what's the point? The point is that man has learned to control the behavior of his fellow man with alarming effectiveness through the use of very immediate but worthless reinforcers. You see the six-month-old baby orient toward the TV screen when the commercials come on. His TV watching behavior is being controlled by the high rate of presentation of reinforcing visual and auditory patterns. He's just like us. The message doesn't matter to him. And it doesn't matter all that much to you or me either. The long range reinforcing value of most of this television viewing is next to nothing; a picture or sound loses its reinforcing power if you are exposed to it for very long. So a "good" TV program gets rid of a sight and sound after just a few seconds (before they lose their reinforcing value) and replaces them with a brand new audio-visual combination. That way, the program remains highly reinforcing for 30 minutes, 60 minutes, even 90 minutes.

S^R (the presentation of sights and sounds that are replaced with new sights and sounds before the old ones lose their reinforcing power)

R (watching TV) ⟶ S^R (large but distant reinforcers)

S^{P*} (the punishing stimuli that seem to accompany any kind of work whether it is digging a ditch or reading a difficult book)

R (doing something constructive)

*"S^P" stands for "punishing stimulus" or simply "punisher".

The major purpose of commercial television is not to inform you, not to educate you, not to make you happy, but simply to reinforce the response of watching television. Of course, it is hoped that you would also watch the commercials and that they would control your purchasing behavior; but for any of that to happen, you must watch the TV in the first place.

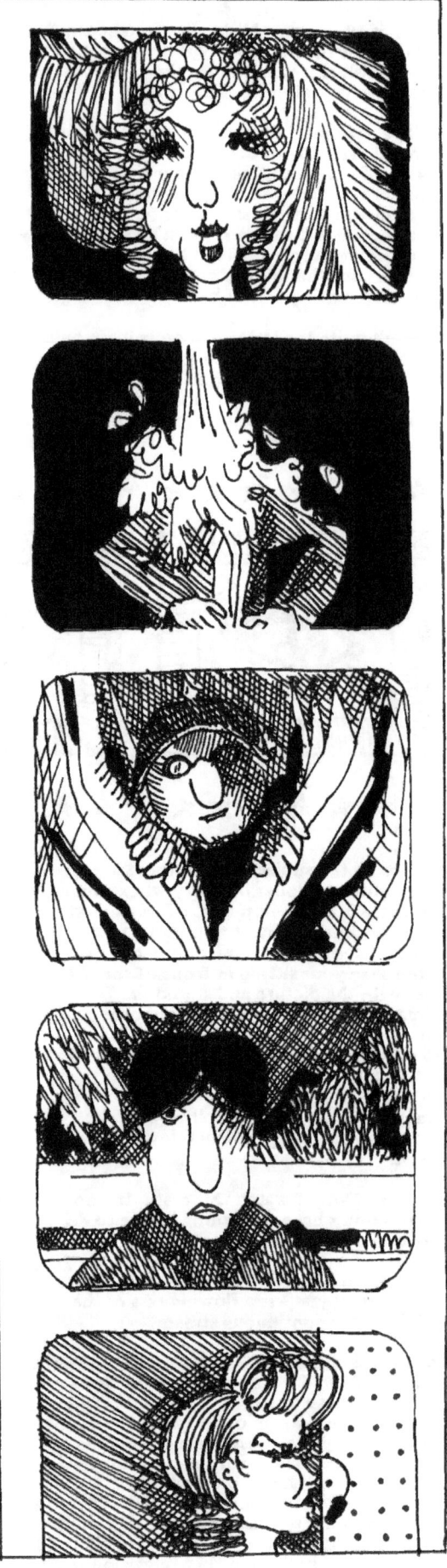

2—11

ENTERTAINMENT

Television is just one form of entertainment, and what we've said about TV is equally true of all other forms. Motion pictures are a good example. The purpose of a motion picture is to reinforce your paying $2.00, picking up your ticket, sitting in front of the screen, looking at the screen for 90 minutes, and then exiting from the building in an orderly manner without demanding your money back. The main purpose of motion pictures is not to end the war in Viet Nam, promote a better understanding among the races, or expose American society as the shallow, brutalizing culture of intolerance it is presumed to be by people who take leisurely motorcycle vacation trips to New Orleans. (Incidentally, the real moral of that beautiful travelogue, **EASY RIDER**, is that if you're a northern freak riding a bike down South and a redneck points a shotgun at you, whatever you do, don't be so stupid as to flip him the bird.)

The same thing is true of paintings. The purpose of a painting is to be such a powerful reinforcer that it will reinforce the sequence of responses beginning with your working hard at your job, getting your pay check, etc., and ending with your pulling a large number of hard-earned dollars out of your billfold and giving them to the salesman at the art gallery.

What about literature? The same thing applies. Language technologists, i. e., professional writers, are very skilled at arranging sequences of words on pages so that the reading response is almost continuously reinforced. And, of course, before you make the reading responses, you've got to make the book purchasing or stealing response.

Comic books are merely attempts to enhance the reinforcing value of the printed page with the inclusion of visual reinforcers. **LIFE MAGAZINE** is produced by people who are expert at using photographs as visual reinforcers for the responses of purchasing and looking at magazines.

Music? You can sing "Power to the People" until you're hoarse, but that's not going to produce a political revolution. Music is a sequence of auditory stimuli that are very reinforcing to hear and even more reinforcing to produce, and that's all. You can increase the reinforcing value by adding visual stimuli such as live musicians and a light show. In fact, adding the visual stimuli can increase the reinforcing value so much that you will pay $4.00 for admission to a rock concert, but you wouldn't pay that amount for a record that you only hear once.

And then there is Art with a capital "A." By this we mean not only painting and sculpture, but also music, dance, theatre, literature, etc. What's the difference between Art and entertainment? Entertainment by any other name is still entertainment. There is no real difference. Art is sights and sounds arranged to be very powerful reinforcers for the looking and listening behavior of "educated" and "cultured" people. Such people would argue that Art has much more than its capacity to reinforce the looking and listening of the connoisseur. They will say that Art is an improving experience; after you have been exposed to Art you will be a better person. Even when this is true, we would suspect that such delayed and improbable reinforcers as self-improvement (either physical or spiritual) must play a very minor role in determining whether the Art is reinforcing enough to keep us looking and listening.

I once had the opportunity to hear political folk
   singer Pete Seeger justify the content of
   his songs by quoting political playwright
   George Bernard Shaw to the effect that
   "All good art is propaganda." As an es-
   thetic generalization that's not too bad,
   but as a political generalization it might
   be better to say: "All good propaganda is
   art." Effective propaganda must contain
   a large enough number of cleverly arranged immediate reinforcers to keep
   you involved. Very few people would be
   aware of Officer Obie's unfashionably
   premature ecological concern for the
   environs of Stockbridge, Massachussetts,
   and its potential implications of a fascist
   police state staffed with Keystone Cops
   who persecuted long-hairs through selective
   law enforcement if political folk-rock
   singer Arlo Guthrie hadn't recorded a
   song about it. But he did, and he was
   very skilled in the use of immediate reinforcers. He dropped those reinforcers
   in there with such casual millisecond
   accuracy that we screamed for more.

"Do you want more, folks?"

"Yes, more."

"Give us a book."

"Give us a movie."

That's good propaganda; that's Art.

Entertainment is a set of immediate reinforcers
   cleverly arranged to keep cultured and
   educated people begging for more.

Art is a set of immediate reinforcers cleverly
   arranged to keep cultured and educated
   people begging for more.

Propaganda is a set of immediate reinforcers
   cleverly arranged to keep you begging
   for more. It is also designed to change
   the way you will behave in the future.

"I don't know why it is, but I feel the
   only person I can vote for for president
   is Yoko Lennon."

Education is a set of immediate punishers
   clumsily arranged to keep you begging
   for less. It is also supposed to change
   the way you will behave in the future.

EDUCATION is the name.
DELAYED REINFORCEMENT is the
   game.

The reinforcement for studying, for learning,
   for getting an education, is usually said to
   lie in the distant future.

"Don't ask me why you should learn this.
   When you're grown up, you'll really
   appreciate the fact that you can read
   Latin."

We know reinforcement in the uncertain future
   competes very poorly with more
   immediate and definite reinforcement.
   And studying competes very poorly with
   entertainment, Art, or propaganda. So
   if you can't beat 'em, imitate 'em. We
   are now experimenting with the use of
   immediate reinforcers developed by the
   entertainment industry. We're trying to
   include enough immediate reinforcers
   in our educational material that study
   behavior will more successfully compete
   with other activities. This is very difficult
   to do without the experience and millions
   of dollars of the entertainment industry,
   but we're making a beginning.

A small step for entertainment but not
   bad for education.

Even traditional educational material has some
   immediate reinforcers built into it. It is
   sometimes reinforcing to read a new idea
   or explanation of something you have
   been curious about but haven't
   understood. But there is more to education than the mere exposure to new ideas.
   You should learn something, and usually
   you should learn it well. That's the hard
   part. We have found that many text
   books contain enough immediate reinforcers to maintain the student's behavior
   of reading the book once. However, with
   only a single reading, very few students
   learned enough to use what they read. If
   a book is worth reading the first time, it
   should be read two or three times so that
   it will be learned well enough to be used.
   Unfortunately, after you have read a book
   once, the little surprises, the new ideas, the
   brilliant explanations are no longer effective reinforcers; and your behavior soon
   comes under the control of more powerful
   immediate reinforcers such as those
   associated with daydreaming or sleeping.

An example: You are a student at the
   LENNY BRUCE SCHOOL OF FAMOUS
   COMEDIANS and you are supposed to
   memorize all of the jokes in your text
   book, 1000 REALLY FUNNY JOKES,
   by G. Hershey. Those punch lines are so
   surprising, the jokes are so funny, that
   those little reinforcers really grab you;
   you read the book cover to cover. Then
   you start to lay a few one-liners on your
   room-mate but forget most of the punch
   lines. You need to read the book again;
   too bad, this time it holds almost no
   immediate reinforcers.

And there you are. One of the many serious
   problems with education is the absence
   of immediate reinforcers.

'TIS THE SEASON TO BE JOLLY

September 1.

Husband: I'm going to put a little aside every two weeks. Then there will be enough money to have a really good Christmas without going into debt to Sears and paying exhorbitant interest rates for another year.

Wife: Let's do the Christmas shopping early this year so we can avoid the rush. There'll also be a wider selection of things to choose from.

November 1.

Husband: I'm going to have to put a good coat of wax on the car before it snows. If I don't, there won't be any car left. The salt they put on these Michigan roads eats 'em right up.

December 1.

Wife: Dear, when are you going to put up the outside tree lights?
Husband: I'll wait until tomorrow when it's a little warmer.

December 24, 11:00 a.m.

Wife: My God, it's crowded here at Sears. I hope we'll be able to get all our shopping done.
Husband: It sure is a good thing we have our charge cards.

December 24, 4:00 p.m.

Wife: When do you think your parents will get here tomorrow?
Husband: Well, you know how they are; they'll probably get us out of bed; they always like to watch the grandchildren unwrap their presents. You remember last Christm......
Wife: Don't bother me now; I've got to get this pie in the oven.
Wise Husband: You know, every time we're preparing to have guests over for a party or a meal, we always get uptight and then start arguing with each other.
Agreeable Wife: Yes, that's dumb. Today, let's not argue.
Worried Husband: I'm afraid Dad may not like the copy of ELEMENTARY PRINCIPLES OF BEHAVIOR I'm giving him for Christmas.
Skeptical Wife: I wonder if you shouldn't have gotten him a new copy; that one looks like it's been through a fraternity hell week.
Concerned Husband: I hope your pie turns out better than the one you baked for Thanksgiving.
Indignant Wife: If you'll stay out of the kitchen so I can get my work done, it might.
Anatomical Husband: If you had half a brain, you'd be able to do a simple job, like baking a pie, and still carry on a decent conversation.
Rapier-witted Wife: If I had someone to carry on a decent conversation with, I probably could.

> There is nothing more immediately reinforcing than bitching at someone you love when you get a little uptight, even though the less probable and distant consequences can be disastrous.

Baby: Wha, Wha, Wha.
Wife: Will you pick the baby up and get her to stop that racket.

Picking up a well-fed, dry and comfortable crying infant is immediately reinforcing to the parent because it terminates the crying. The long-range consequences are not so good, however, since being picked up is a very powerful reinforcer for the infant's crying response. Therefore, crying is even more likely to occur in the future. If the parents are sure everything is cool, they should ignore crying behavior.

Wife: You really ought to get started on those toys. You know how long it took you last year when you had to put together that easy-to-assemble-just-follow-the-simple-illustrated-instructions cardboard doll house and complete kitchen set. And this year there are even more toys for you to assemble.
Husband: I'll get on it just as soon as Walter Cronkite is over.

December 24, 11:00 p.m.

Husband: Well, I finally put those Christmas lights on the shrubs outside. Ya' know, I think it looks even better than last year. But damn, it's cold. I could use a good stiff drink before we go to bed.
Wife: But don't forget about those toys. You still have to put them together. I'm going to be staying up, too. I have to wrap all the packages.

December 25, 3:00 a.m.

Wife: Finally, the last package; and am I ever ready for bed!
Husband: I'll join you.
Wife: But you haven't finished assembling Junior's new polystyrene intergalactic spaceship and floating brothel.
Husband: I'm going to wait until tomorrow. A father and son working side-by-side on such a project build more than a plastic toy; they also build family unity.

December 25, 6:00 a.m.

Husband: Huh...aah...umph...Wha da ya want? Can't you see I'm trying to sleep? Get the hell out of here.
Child: Daddy, Daddy, it's Christmas! It's time to unwrap the presents!
Daddy: Ahh...oh...Merry Christmas. O.K., let's go do it.

December 30, any time.

Husband: Every time we go to a party, we always arrive late because you spend so much time getting ready. Now tomorrow night I'd like to arrive on time at the New Year's Eve Party. Why don't you start getting ready an hour early so we can do that.
Wife: If you had to fix supper, clean up the kitchen, and put the kids to bed, you'd know why I can't start getting ready early.
Husband: Well, I hate sitting around for an hour all dressed up just so I can wait for you to get ready. Why don't you tell me now when you plan to be ready to leave.?
Wife: O.K. I'll be ready by nine o'clock.

December 31, 9:45 p.m.

Husband: At last, you're ready. I don't know why you can't ever be on time. Let's get the hell out of here.
Wife: You don't have to be such a grouch; it's not all that important.

December 31, 9:50 p.m.

Husband: Look at that gas gauge. The needle's pointing to "E"; we're almost out of gas. How many times have I told you never to let the tank get that low.
Wife: We probably won't run out of gas before we get to the station. By the way, we've had snow on the roads for the last five weeks and you still haven't waxed the car.
Husband: I've been meaning to get around to it, but I've been so darned busy. I've got to get this car serviced, too; it's nearly 1000 miles overdue. I'd feel a lot better if you'd fasten your seat belt.
Wife: So would I, but it's all tangled. Besides, if you'd just drive at a more reasonable speed, you wouldn't have to worry about me.
Husband: If those greedy capitalists in Detroit would worry less about profit and more about automotive safety, this car would be safe at any speed.
Wife: Sure, but you know yourself that CONSUMER'S GLOOMER rated this car as one of the biggest safety hazards on the highway. And yet you went ahead and bought it.
Husband: Yeah, but it's a really sharp looking car. Those fat-cat capitalists make me mad anyway with their lack of concern for public health and safety — all that pollution and smog and smoke. Say, that reminds me, did you bring an extra pack of cigarettes? What was the address of that party again?
Wife: Just a second...It's 96 Shambling Road.
Husband: Damn it! I think we missed our turn. I don't know this part of town very well.
Wife: Now we're really going to be late and it's all your fault. If you'd be less concerned about reforming Detroit and pay more attention to where you're driving, this wouldn't have happened.
Husband: You're not blind, you know. You could be keeping an eye out for the road signs. I don't think that would be asking too much.
Wife: (ah, sweet revenge) If you had half a brain, you'd be able to do a simple job like driving a car and still be able to carry on a civil conversation.
Husband (with an equal lack of originality): If I had someone to carry on a civil conversation with, I probably could.
Author (with an equal lack of originality): There is nothing more immediately reinforcing than bitching at someone you love when you get a little uptight, even though the less probable and distant consequences can be disastrous. Show me a student with parents, and I'll show you a child who rode in the back seat and couldn't figure out why mom and dad always got into a fight when they got lost. "Boy, that sure is a stupid argument; boy, I'll never do anything that stupid when I grow up and get married." Everyone thinks his parents were the only ones who got into those kinds of hassles...Not true.

December 31, 11:55 p.m.

Husband: My New Year's resolutions are that I'll start putting a little money aside for next Christmas; I'll stop procrastinating on things like waxing and servicing the car, putting up tree lights, and assembling the toys; I'll stop hassling you when I get uptight; I'll stop smoking; and I'll even stop speeding; but I'm not going to trade my car in on a safer model.
Wife: And I'll stop procrastinating on things like Christmas shopping, keeping the gas tank filled, and getting ready for parties; I'll stop bitching at you when I get uptight; I'll stop smoking; and I'll stop picking up the baby every time she cries.
Husband: Gosh, I feel better already.
Wife: Me too. I feel positively moral.
Husband and Wife: Happy New Year!

March 20.

Wife: Honey, when are you going to take down those outside Christmas lights?

RECAP

1. Perhaps the most important message of this chapter is the title itself. It describes the way that behavioral psychologists look at behavior, including problem behavior. For example, if a child has frequent temper tantrums, his problem is almost certainly not some underlying disease that erupts into tantrums, nor is his problem a manifestation of any mental disorder. His problem is that he has too many tantrums — an external problem with an external cause. Which is to say that environmental contingencies have been so arranged that the child received a great deal of reinforcement from his environment when he had a temper tantrum.

2. Behaviorists have many other beliefs that are consistent with the notion that YA'ARE WHA'CHA DO. They are determinists because they believe that behavior has a cause. They are environmentalists because they believe that most of the causes of man's behavior can be found in his environment. They are learning theorists because they believe that environment causes behavior by teaching man to behave the way he does. They are reinforcement theorists because they believe that the environment teaches man to behave the way he does by consequating his behavior. They are perfectionists because if man's behavior is taught by his environment, an optimal environmental arrangement would result in man's behavior reaching its optimal level. They are realists because they realize that arranging an optimal environment is extremely difficult, if not impossible.

3. Our culture has established many of our personal goals and needs for us. However, the contingencies arranged by the culture often fail to help us reach these goals or ideals. The primary controlling powers of our culture usually are in the form of social pressure. We do what we do because our friends or parents approve or disapprove of our behavior. They approve or disapprove as our behavior resembles or fails to resemble the cultural ideals. This social pressure would probably be enough to control most behavior if it were used frequently and consistently. However, we typically are punished when we fail to achieve these goals but receive little reinforcement or punishment along the way. Problems arise in the control of behavior when more frequent reinforcers are made available for undesirable behavior. For example, our culture teaches us that it is good to lead a long, healthy life. However, few "baddies" are forthcoming for the person who overeats — until it is too late. On the other hand, that person receives frequent, immediate reinforcement for overeating — the taste of all that food. Typically, our culture assumes that goals and ideals are enough to control behavior, but frequently that assumption is wrong. When people do achieve their culture's goals, it is usually due to the presence of more immediate consequences for "appropriate" behavior: consequences which come from parents, peer groups with the same goals, teachers, employers, etc. What we are concerned with is how to arrange our environment so that more people may attain those goals specified by their culture.

4. Behavior is influenced by its consequences, and there are many potential consequences for one's behavior. The consequences that are most effective in controlling behavior are those consequences that are immediate and certain. A consequence that occurs only once out of 100 times won't control much behavior.

OBJECTIVES

1. If you believe that behavior is the subject matter of psychology, you are a(n) _____.
   a) practitioner
   b) realist
   c) behaviorist
   d) determinist
   e) empiricist

2. _____ believe(s) that man's behavior is caused.
   a) Determinists
   b) The Pope
   c) Causationists
   d) Environmentalists
   e) All psychologists

3. Environmentalists (in psychology) believe that _____.
   a) we should all take care of our environment
   b) man's behavior is not affected by his environment
   c) we must conquer our environment before it conquers us
   d) all consumables should be packaged in bio-degradable containers
   e. man's behavior is controlled by his environment

4. Learning theorists believe that man's behavior is a product of _____.
   a) genetics
   b) divine intervention
   c) innate programs present in DNA molecules
   d) his interaction with his environment.
   e) a & c

5. Those who believe that future behavior is influenced by the RESULTS of present behavior are called _____.
   a) environmentalists
   b) perfectionists
   c) realists
   d) reinforcement theorists
   e) determinists

6. Perfectionists believe that man can approximate perfection through _____.
   a) genetics
   b) natural selection (survival of the fittest)
   c) arranging his environment so that it reinforces desirable behavior
   d) a & b
   e) all of the above

7. Behavior is more easily influenced by _____ than by _____.
   a) small immediate reinforcers; large distant reinforcers
   b) genetics; reinforcement
   c) thought processes; genetics
   d) stimuli; reinforcers
   e) small, immediate reinforcers; large, immediate reinforcers

8. The probability of future responses is influenced by _____.
   a) reinforcement
   b) punishment
   c) extinction
   d) a & b
   e) all of the above

9. The probability of future responses is increased by _____.
   a) positive reinforcement
   b) negative reinforcement
   c) punishment
   d) a & b
   e) all of the above

10. Reinforcer effectiveness is determined by:
    a) the immediacy of its presentation following the behavior
    b) the recipient's I. Q.
    c) the degree of certainty (probability) that the reinforcer will be presented following a response
    d) a & c
    e) all of the above

11. The probability of future responses is decreased by _____.
    a) positive reinforcement
    b) negative reinforcement
    c) punishment
    d) conditioning
    e) b & c

12. A consequence is a stimulus that can be _____.
    a) neutral
    b) punishing
    c) reinforcing
    d) b & c
    e) all of the above

ANSWERS

1. c; 2. a; 3. e; 4. d; 5. d; 6. c; 7. a; 8. e; 9. d; 10. d; 11. c; 12. e.

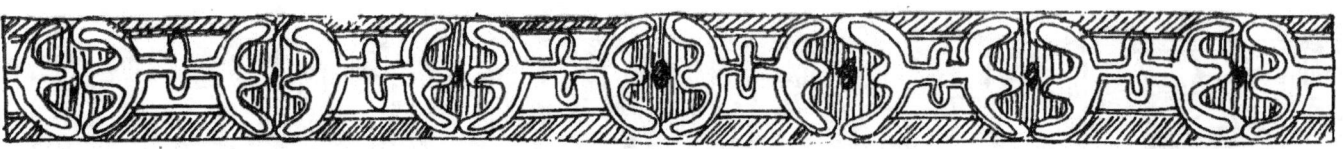

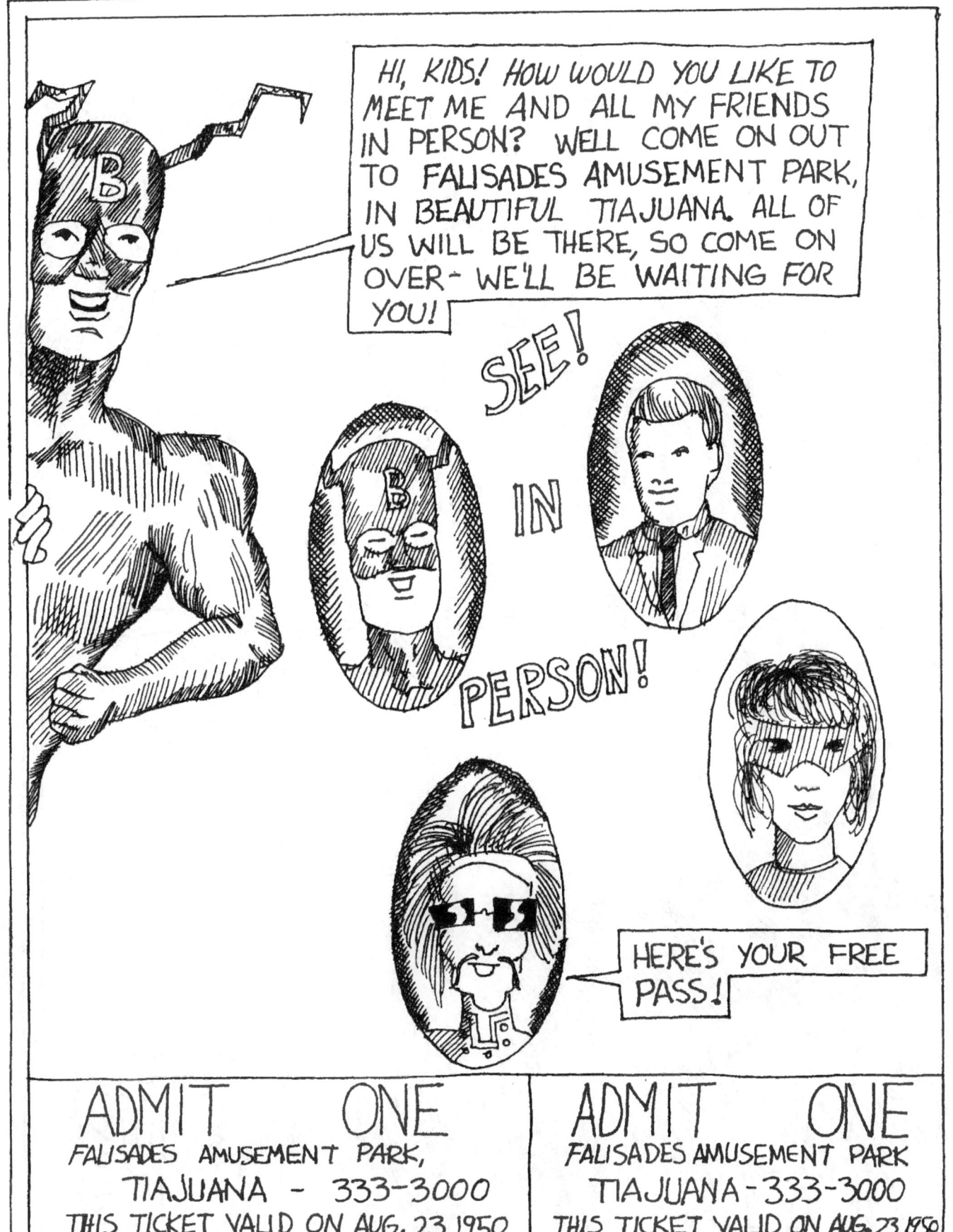

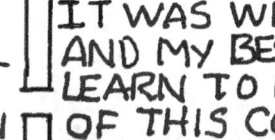

"LEARNING TO READ BETTER SHOULD BE ALL OF THE P_____ REINFORCE_____ THEY NEED. LEARNING SHOULD BE ITS OWN REWARD."

"IF LEARNING WERE ITS OWN REIN_____ OUR JOB WOULD BE A LOT EASIER, BUT IT'S NOT."

"IT WAS WHEN I WAS A CHILD, AND MY BEST STUDENTS STILL LEARN TO READ WITHOUT ANY OF THIS CODDLING."

"THE REAL QUESTION IS NOT 'WHY DOES JOHNNY FAIL,' IT IS 'WHY DOES SALLY LEARN?' IT'S A WONDER ANYONE LEARNS TO READ."

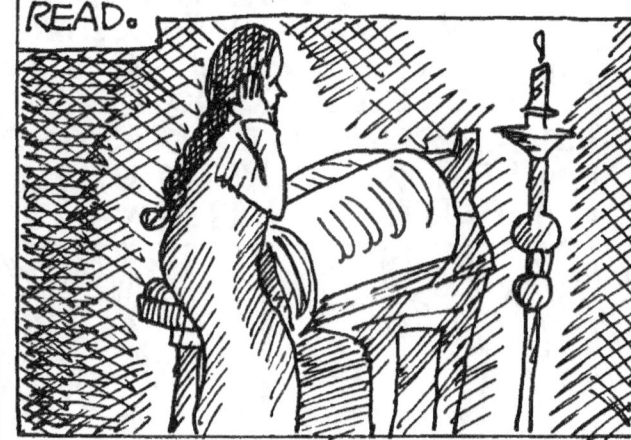

"INDEED IT IS. FORTUNATELY, SOME KIDS DO HAVE THE BEHAVIORAL PREREQUISITES FOR LEARNING TO READ.
1. THEY HAVE LEARNED TO FOLLOW INSTRUCTIONS.
2. THEY HAVE LEARNED TO STAY WITH A TASK FOR A RESONABLE PERIOD OF TIME.
3. THERE ARE VARIOUS EVENTS CONTINGENT ON READING WHICH HAVE ACQUIRED REINFORCING POWER FOR THEM."

IN MOST SITUATIONS, A CHOCOLATE MALT, A PLAYBOY MAGAZINE, A BEAUTIFUL SUNSET, A JOE COCKER RECORD, AND MY WARM, AFFECTIONATE SMILE ARE P_____ R_____. TO PUT IT ROUGHLY, GETTING A GOODIE FOR DOING SOMETHING IS CALLED POSITIVE REINFORCEMENT. AND ESCAPING A BADDIE IS CALLED NEGATIVE _____.

SUPPOSE YOU GET CAUGHT IN THE RAIN AND RUN INDOORS. WHAT IS THAT SITUATION CALLED?

THAT IS NEGATIVE REINFORCEMENT, BECAUSE I ESCAPED A BADDIE, A NEGATIVE REINFORCER.

WELL, SOME THINGS LIKE FOOD, WATER AND SEX...

GASP!

I DIDN'T MEAN TO SHOCK YOUR SENSIBILITIES, MISS. LET'S JUST STICK TO FOOD AND WATER. WELL, SOME THINGS LIKE FOOD AND WATER ARE BASIC, UNLEARNED REINFORCERS. WE CALL THEM PRIMARY REINFORCERS.

OTHER THINGS LIKE MONEY AND SOCIAL APPROVAL ARE LEARNED REINFORCERS. WE CALL THEM SECONDARY REINFORCERS.

MONEY BECOMES A REINFORCER ONLY AFTER WE LEARN THAT WE CAN BUY FOOD AND OTHER GOODIES WITH IT. IN THE SAME WAY, SOCIAL APPROVAL BECOMES A REINFORCER ONLY AFTER WE LEARN THAT PEOPLE WILL BE MORE LIKELY TO GIVE US FOOD AND OTHER GOODIES IF WE HAVE THEIR APPROVAL.

MOTHER

We're nearly always on a CONCURRENT SCHEDULE OF REINFORCEMENT. At any one time there's a wide variety of responses we can make. And various reinforcers are contingent upon many of these responses. The response we make is determined by our history of reinforcement with these competing responses and by the strength of the various reinforcers.

This may be true of little kids, but surely a mature adult is free to choose the response which is in his own best interest.

Let's put it this way: which response a mature adult "chooses" is a result of his history of reinforcement with those responses and the strength of the various reinforcers concurrently available for those responses.

3-28

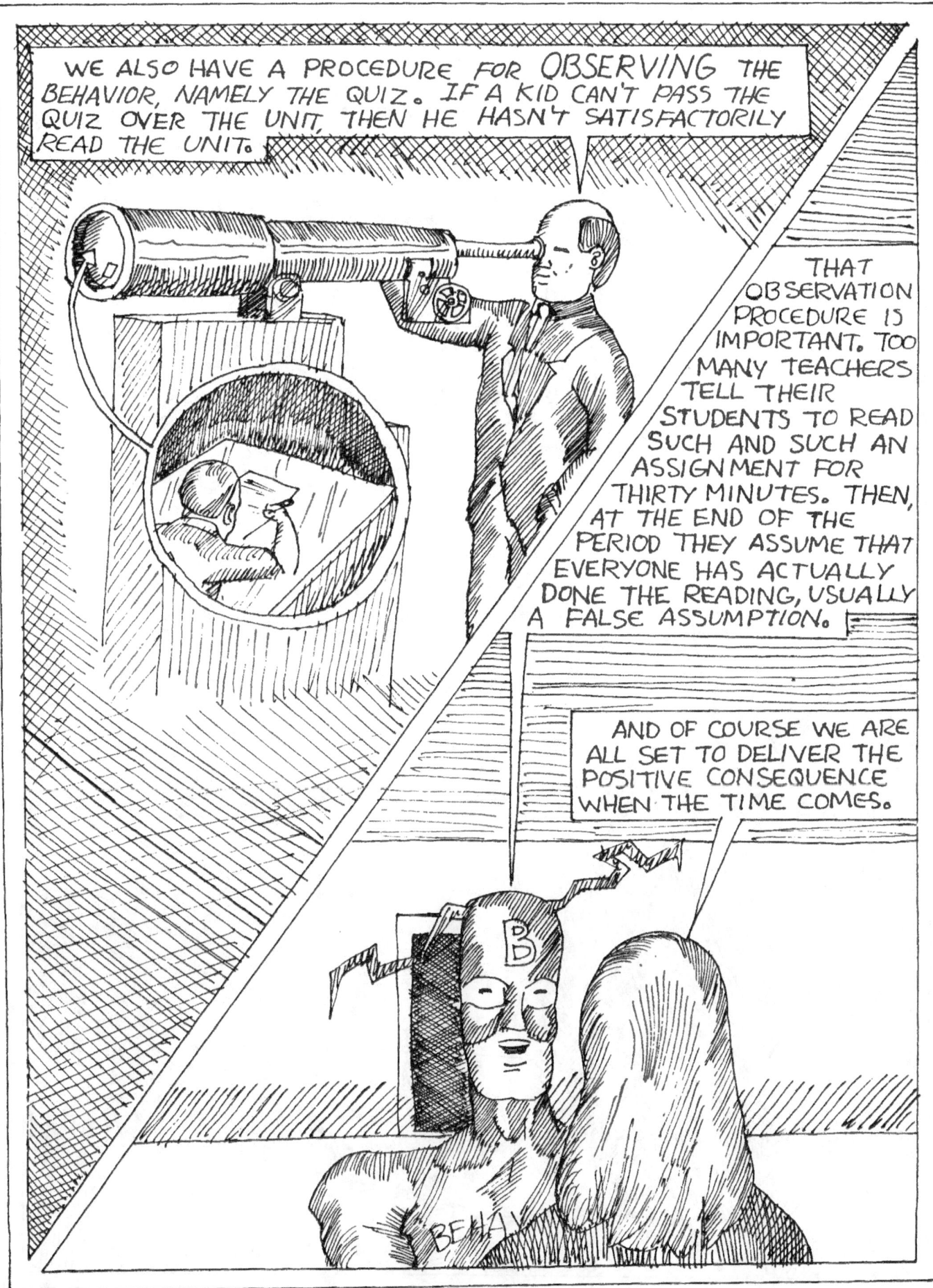

RECAP

1. The previous chapter introduced the first rule of contingency management, be consistent. Four additional rules are presented in this chapter: think small, establish functional behavior, start where the behavior is at, and reinforce each unit of the stimulus-response chain.

2. The "think small" rule is important for two reasons:
   a. It allows administrators to concentrate resources on smaller areas, and thus deal more effectively with those areas.
   b. It allows the subjects to concentrate their behavior on smaller areas, learning fewer things but learning them to a high level of competence.

3. "Establishing functional behavior" is important because the behavior changes made in the controlled environment should be maintained in a non-controlled environment. Functional behavior is behavior that will be reinforced by the subject's natural environment, peer group, etc.

4. To "start where the behavior is at" means to consider prerequisite behavior. It would be foolish to attempt to teach calculus to students who were no further than subtraction.

5. "Reinforcing each unit of the stimulus-response chain" is providing immediate consequences for behavior. After each response, feedback is provided, thus strengthening correct responses and weakening incorrect responses.

6. The previous chapter also said that a contingency was the relationship between a behavior and its consequence. There are four basic contingencies.
   a. positive reinforcement — a positive reinforcer is presented after the behavior is emitted.
   b. negative reinforcement — a negative reinforcer is removed after the behavior is emitted.
   c. avoidance — the presentation of an aversive event is delayed or prevented as a consequence of the desired behavior.
   d. punishment — an aversive event is presented after the behavior is emitted.
   Positive reinforcement, negative reinforcement, and avoidance are all followed by increased response probabilities, and punishment results in a decreased response probability.

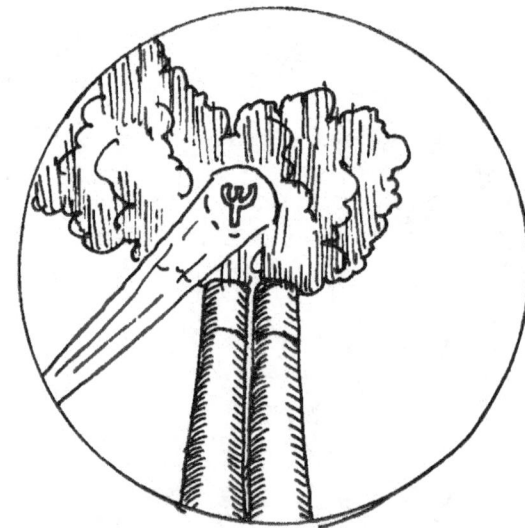

7. The concurrent schedule of reinforcement mentioned by Behaviorman suggests the complexity of behavior and its analysis. It is sometimes overlooked that behavior can be simultaneously controlled by many variables. A concurrent schedule is when a variety of responses at any given time can result in one or more reinforcers.

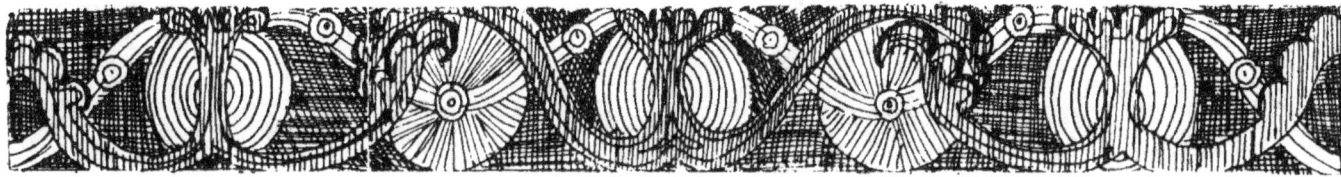

OBJECTIVES

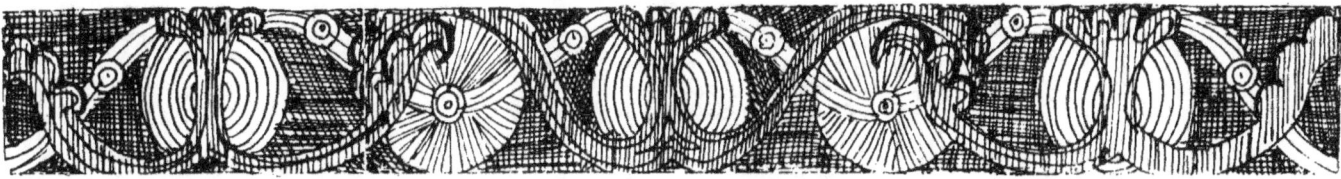

1. What is the first rule of contingency management?
   a) Be consistent (nothing in moderation)
   b) Be prepared
   c) Plan ahead
   d) Be lenient

2. What is the second rule of contingency management?
   a) Plan ahead
   b) Increase work load
   c) Think small
   d) Think big

3. Why is it better to concentrate on only one subject or area rather than a wide range of subjects?
   a) to produce a strong program in at least that one area
   b) to have a better chance of modifying that particular behavior
   c) to reduce the work load of the teacher
   d) a & b.
   e) all of the above

4. What is the third rule of contingency management?
   a) Love thy neighbor
   b) Establish functional behavior
   c) Become aware of the problems surrounding the behavior
   d) Establish a serious atmosphere

5. Why is the third rule of contingency management so important?
   a) By showing the subject the relationship between behavior and the reinforcers, he will be more apt to realize the importance of appropriate behavior
   b) So that there is something between the second and fourth rules
   c) To keep the subject interested
   d) The subject must be able to obtain reinforcers outside of the contingency management environment so that the desired behavior won't extinguish

6. The fourth rule of contingency management is:
   a) Start where the behavior is at
   b) Reinforce only acceptable behavior
   c) Combine reinforcement and punishment where possible
   d) Choose the correct reinforcement schedule

7. Which of the following is NOT a behavioral prerequisite for learning to read?
   a) learning to follow instructions
   b) learning to stay with a task for a reasonable amount of time
   c) properties of reading have acquired reinforcing power
   d) eyesight

8. What is the most powerful secondary reinforcer known to man?
   a) food
   b) free time
   c) social approval
   d) sex
   e) poetry

9. If a positive reinforcer follows a response, what happens to the probability of that response?
   a) It increases
   b) It decreases
   c) It remains constant
   d) One cannot predict what will happen

10. Which of the following is NOT one of the four basic contingencies of contingency management?
    a) positive reinforcement
    b) neutral reinforcement
    c) negative reinforcement
    d) avoidance
    e) punishment

11. What are the basic unlearned reinforcers called?
    a) innate reinforcers
    b) primary reinforcers
    c) secondary reinforcers
    d) conditioned reinforcers

12. How does something become a secondary reinforcer?

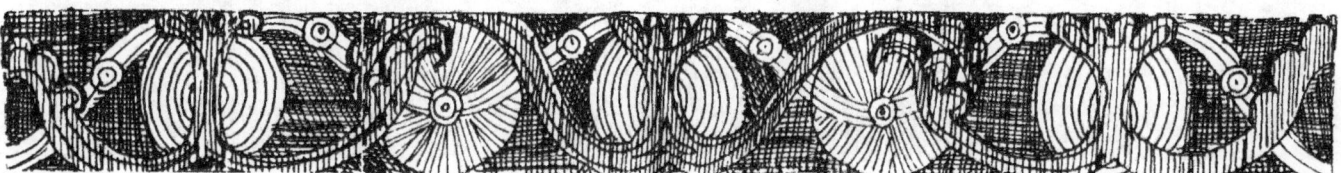

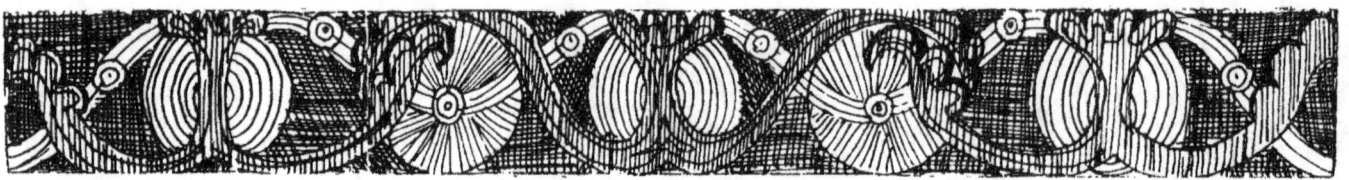

a) by eliminating the primary reinforcer
b) by being associated with a wide variety of punishers
c) by being made contingent upon appropriate behavior
d) by being associated with a primary reinforcer

13. What is the fifth rule of contingency management?
    a) Reinforce each unit of the stimulus-response chain.
    b) Reinforce all behaviors so that the desired behavior won't extinguish.
    c) Eliminate all irrelevant stimuli.
    d) Encourage all subjects (students) to work at the same rate, thereby encouraging competition.

14. What is the primary purpose for isolating the student in a study booth?
    a) to punish unruly or disruptive students
    b) to reduce the student-faculty ratio
    c) to learn to study alone
    d) to eliminate sources of reinforcement for behavior that competes with reading (studying)

15. What is a stimulus-response chain?
    a) a sequence of stimuli and responses
    b) a sequence of positive and negative reinforcers
    c) a sequence of punishers and reinforcers
    d) the procedure of reinforcing only the desired behavior while not reinforcing any other behavior

16. What are the three essential features of a good contingency management program? (Choose three answers.)
    a) Specify the consequences
    b) Specify the behavior
    c) Specify the preceding conditions
    d) Specify the contingency
    e) Specify the inappropriate stimuli verbally

ANSWERS

1. a; 2. c; 3. d; 4. b; 5. d; 6. a; 7. d; 8. c; 9. a; 10. b; 11. b; 12. d; 13. a; 14. d; 15. a; 16. a, b, d.

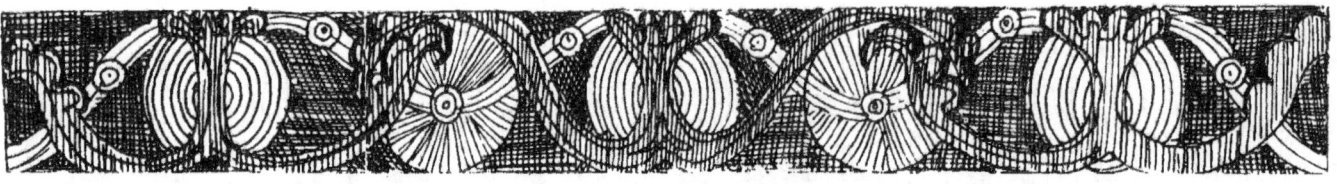

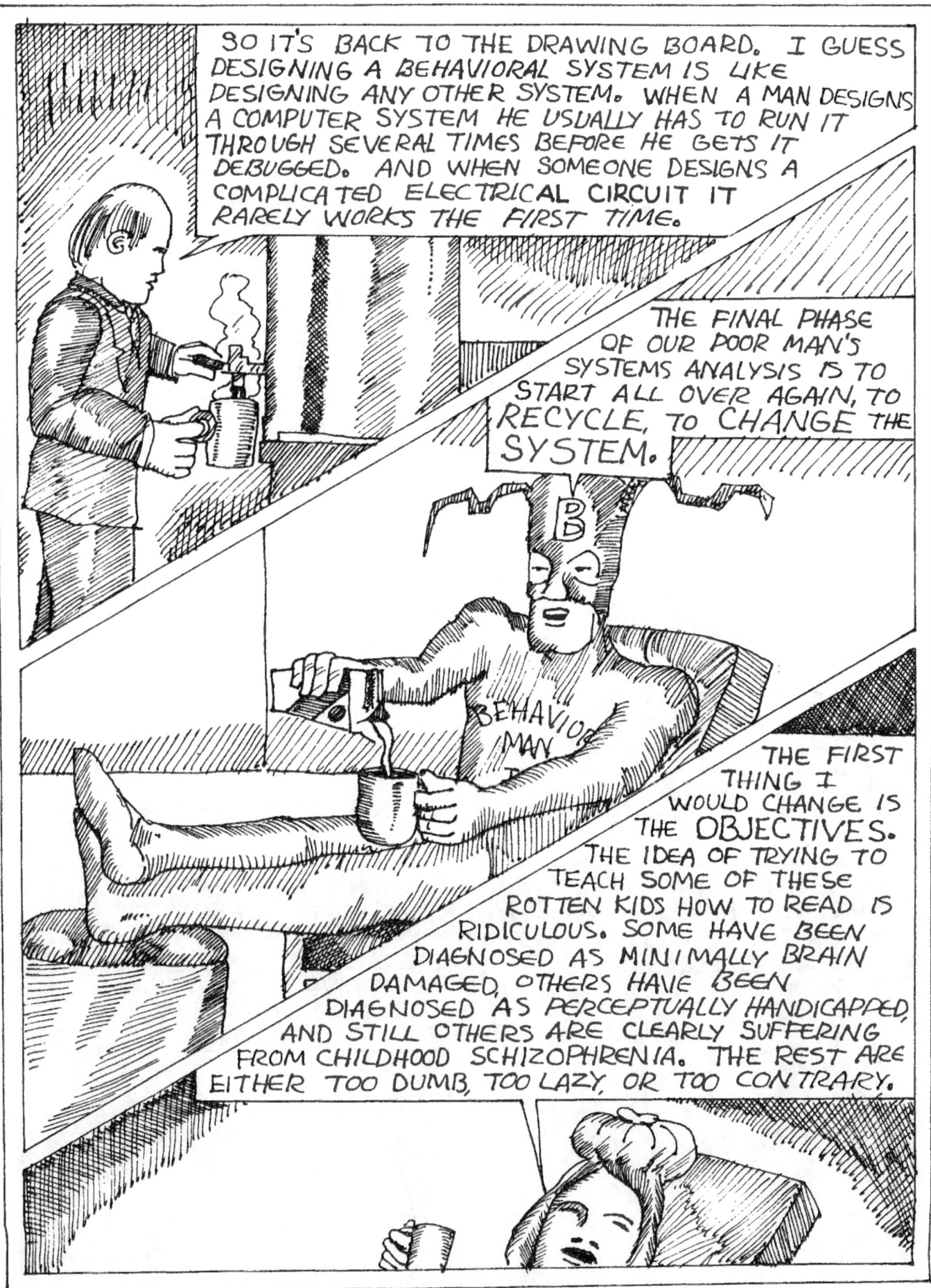

We can divide the S_____ R_____ C____ of reading into units which are even smaller than the reading of a single page, and they may be easier to deal with. The kid's first response is to sit at his desk, the next response is to look at the appropriate page in his book, and the final response in this chain is to read the page.

If he doesn't make the first two responses, he sure as hell can't make the third.

So maybe we should concentrate on those first two responses. Let's make our reinforcers contingent on the kid's actually sticking to the task.

That may be too complicated.

I've got a wild notion that might make it simpler. Let's observe the behavior of the whole class as if it were a single kid. When the entire class has been working industriously for five minutes, then the reinforcement can be delivered to the group as a whole. They can all go out to play. Get an electric clock and put a switch on it.

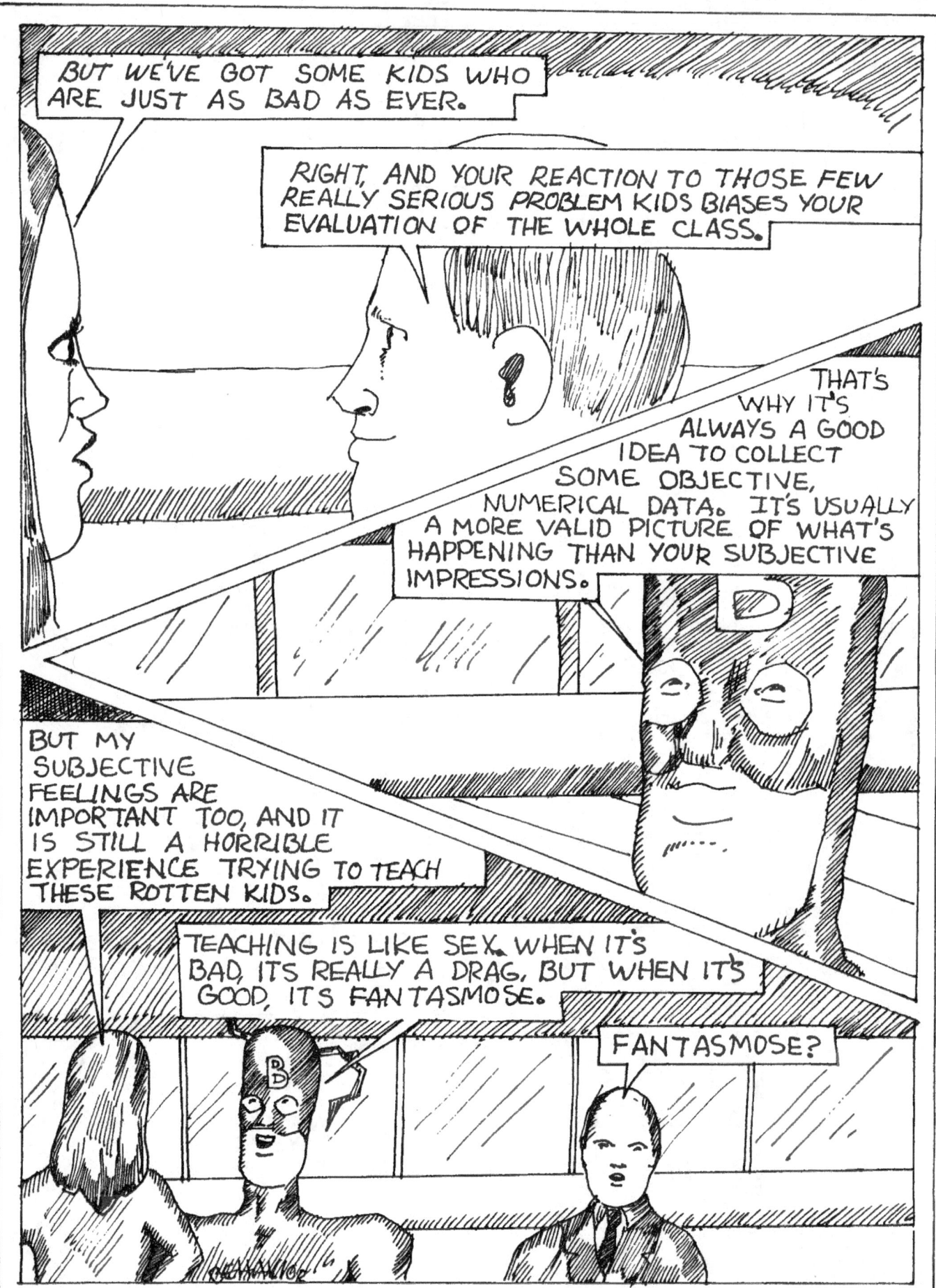

IN FACT, MISS TRADITION AND HER AID, MISS HELPFUL, WERE SLOWING DOWN MORE THAN THE STUDENTS.

THAT'S BECAUSE *NOBODY* WAS GIVING US SNIRKLES.

ANOTHER INTERESTING OBSERVATION IS THAT THE KIDS DON'T START GOOFING OFF AT THE END OF THE DAY LIKE THEY DO IN REGULAR CLASSROOMS.

IT'S HARD TO BELIEVE THAT THESE ARE KIDS WHO WERE REFERRED TO US BECAUSE THEY COULDN'T WORK AND HAD SHORT ATTENTION SPANS.

YES, A GREAT DEAL OF OUR BEHAVIOR IS UNDER THE CONTROL OF THE IMMEDIATE REINFORCING CONSEQUENCES AND INDEPENDENT OF OUR PAST HISTORIES OF REINFORCEMENT. WHEN THE KIDS ARE IN A ROTTEN ENVIRONMENT, THEY'LL ACT LIKE ROTTEN KIDS, BUT WHEN THEY'RE IN A RIGHTEOUS ENVIRONMENT THEY'LL ACT LIKE RIGHTEOUS KIDS.

BUT IF OUR ROTTEN KIDS CANNOT ADAPT TO THEIR NORMAL CLASSROOM ENVIRONMENT, MAYBE ALL OF OUR CONTINGENCY MANAGEMENT IS NOTHING MORE THAN A CRUTCH FOR THE WEAK. MAYBE OUR KIDS ARE BECOMING DEPENDENT ON THE CRUTCH OF CONTINGENCY MANAGEMENT AND WILL HAVE AN EVEN MORE DIFFICULT TIME OF IT WHEN THAT CRUTCH IS REMOVED.

YOUR CONTINGENCY-MANAGEMENT-IS-JUST-LIKE-A-CRUTCH ANALOGY IS NOT APT. THAT'S LIKE SAYING THAT GOOD NUTRITION IS A CRUTCH, THAT PEOPLE SHOULD BE HEALTHY EVEN IF THEY HAVE POOR DIETS.

CAUGHT HIM STARVIN' IN PUBLIC, YER HONER!

OF COURSE, FOR VARIOUS REASONS, SOME PEOPLE WILL BE HARMED MORE BY A POOR DIET THAN WILL OTHERS. AND SOME PEOPLE WILL BE HARMED MORE BY A POOR SET OF CONTINGENCIES THAN WILL OTHERS. BUT GOOD CONTINGENCY MANAGEMENT RESULTS IN GOOD BEHAVIOR, JUST LIKE GOOD NUTRITION RESULTS IN GOOD HEALTH.

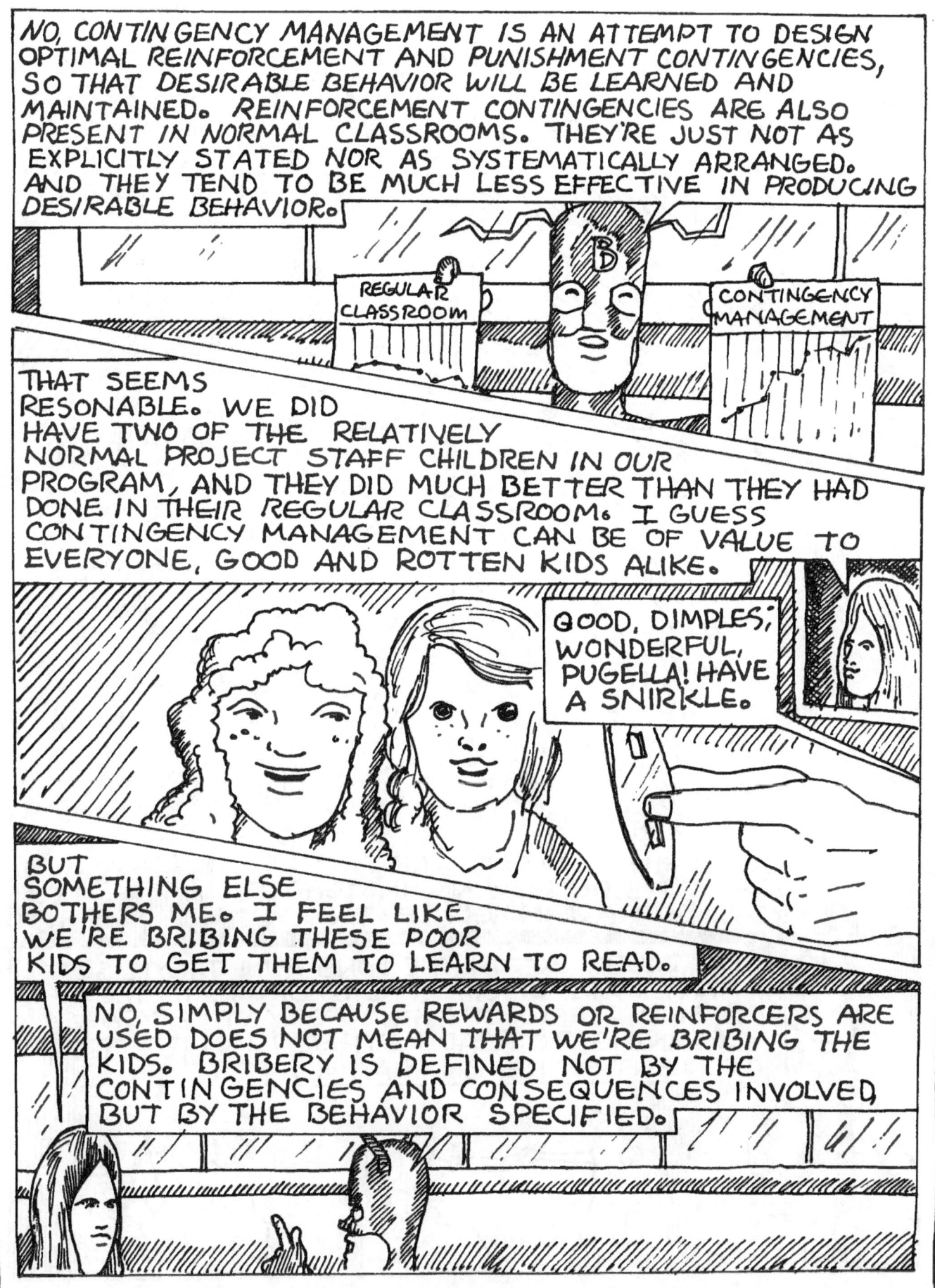

RECAP

1. The phases of systems analysis are: specify the objectives, design the system, implement the system, test the system empirically, recycle the system if necessary; the phases constitute the empirical approach of systems analysis and are necessary for a scientific approach to the analysis of behavior.

2. The Premack Principle states that a preferred activity can be used as a reinforcer for a less preferred activity. Both the preferred and the less preferred activity can be empirically determined. This principle may be applied to any two behaviors that occur at different rates. The opportunity to engage in the behavior with the higher rate can be used as a reinforcer for emitting the behavior with the lower rate.

3. In the previous chapter, one of the rules of contingency management was to "start where the behavior is at." An equally important rule to keep in mind is to "stay where the behavior is at." This doesn't mean that you should never expect more from a student; it means to be careful not to advance your expectations too quickly. If the criterion for reinforcement is advanced too rapidly, the behavior will extinguish. The reinforcement criterion must remain at a level the student can reach.

4. Punishment was defined earlier as the presentation of an aversive event after a response, with a resultant decrease in the rate of that response. The aversive event mentioned can take either of two forms: the presentation of an aversive stimulus (a punisher), or the removal of a positive reinforcer. Thus, punishment can be either the presentation of a punisher or the removal of positive reinforcers.

5. In this chapter, Behaviorman illustrates why the distinction between reward and reinforcer was made in Chapter 1. It is part of an attempt to eliminate subjective interpretations in psychology and take an empirical approach to the analysis of behavior. Miss Tradition assumed that her scoldings were punishing to the students when her scoldings actually increased the rate of the behaviors which she scolded. Since the behavior rate increased, we know that her attention (scolding) was a reinforcer, not a punisher. When analyzing behavior, you must look at the behavior and its results and define those results as reinforcers or punishers in terms of their effect on behavior rather than in terms of your subjective interpretations.

OBJECTIVES

1. The Premack Principle is:
   a) A preferred activity can be used as a punisher for a less preferred activity
   b) A less preferred activity can be used as a reinforcer for a preferred activity
   c) A preferred activity can be used as a reinforcer for a less preferred activity
   d) Any activity can be used as a reinforcer for any other activity
   e) Activities can't be used as reinforcers; therefore, none of the above is true

2. Shaping is the same as:
   a) successive approximations
   b) the procedure (method) of successive approximations
   c) differential reinforcement
   d) a & b

3. Shaping consists of differentially reinforcing successive approximations of behavior toward some terminal behavior. Therefore, the method of successive approximations consists of differentially reinforcing _____ toward some terminal behavior.
   a) successive approximations of behavior
   b) the same response
   c) students
   d) a & b
   e) none of the above

4. "Successive approximations of behavior" refers to:
   a) a method like shaping
   b) small changes of the response topography
   c) differential reinforcement of successive approximations
   d) a & c
   e) something that's close to behavior

5. In the conditioning of a response, reinforcement should be delivered contingent on _____.
   a) the desired behavior
   b) a set number of responses
   c) a variable amount of time
   d) any behavior
   e) shaping

6. If you wish to condition behavior "A" in a subject, reinforcement must be contingent upon _____.
   a) successive approximations
   b) behavior "A"
   c) active responding
   d) small steps
   e) all of the above

7. Contingencies always have an immediate effect on behavior.
   a) True
   b) False
   c) None of the above

8. Removal of a positive reinforcer contingent on a behavior is a _____ contingency.
   a) escape
   b) avoidance
   c) positive reinforcement
   d) negative reinforcement
   e) punishment

9. Objective data is _____ valid than subjective impressions.
   a) more
   b) less
   c) sometimes more and sometimes less

10. Contingency Management is really easy once you know the basic fundamental concepts.
    a) True
    b) False

11. Sometimes it is necessary to _____ competing behaviors before the intended reinforcers will affect behavior.
    a) strengthen
    b) eliminate
    c) shape
    d) reinforce
    e) recognize

12. Competing behaviors are behaviors that are _____ the desired behavior.
    a) strengthened by
    b) compatible with

    c) incompatible with
    d) helpful while conditioning

13. Discipline problems are decreased when undesirable behaviors are _____ and _____ (is/are) made available for the desirable behavior.
    a) strengthened
    b) weakened
    c) reinforcers
    d) other behaviors
    e) observed

14. Contingency management does not affect the behavior of which of the following groups of children?
    a) psychotic
    b) minimally brain damaged
    c) perceptually handicapped
    d) incorrigible
    e) contingency management works with all of the above

15. Behavior is under the control of _____.
    a) our past histories of reinforcement
    b) immediate reinforcing consequences
    c) the environment
    d) b & c
    e) all of the above

16. To change behavior, don't change the individual, change the _____.
    a) past histories of reinforcement
    b) observation
    c) environment
    d) man
    e) none of the above

17. If the behavior is wrong or immoral, then the use of positive reinforcement to get it to occur is _____.
    a) bribery
    b) Contingency Management

18. If the behavior is good and moral, then the use of positive reinforcement to get it to occur is _____.
    a) bribery
    b) Contingency Management

19. The attempt to design optimal reinforcement and punishment contingencies so that desirable behavior will be learned and maintained is called _____.
    a) bribery
    b) Contingency Management
    c) blackmail
    d) conditioning
    e) a & c

ANSWERS

1. c; 2. b; 3. a; 4. b; 5. a; 6. b; 7. b; 8. e; 9. a; 10. b; 11. b; 12. c; 13. b, c (in that order) 14. e; 15. e; 16. c; 17. a; 18. b; 19. b.

Summary – Part 1

Principles of Behavior

SUMMARY — PART 1 (PRINCIPLES OF BEHAVIOR)

CONCEPTS: the following technical terms are relevant to this chapter.

BEHAVIORAL CONSEQUENCE: the results or consequences of the response or behavior. This concept is particularly important since the consequences of behavior are the primary factor in determining whether that behavior will be repeated in the future. There are three basic types of behavioral consequences:

REINFORCER (reinforcing consequence): an event which INCREASES the frequency of the response or behavior it follows. If a response is followed by reinforcing consequences, it will probably be repeated in the future. A "reinforcer" is roughly the same thing as a "reward." However, things sometimes get a little confusing if you insist in always interpreting a "reinforcer" as a "reward."

PUNISHER (punishing consequence): an event which DECREASES the frequency of the response or behavior it follows.

NEUTRAL CONSEQUENCE: an event which has NO EFFECT on the frequency of the behavior it follows. The only reason we mention this is so you know we covered all of the possibilities.

There are two types of reinforcers:

POSITIVE REINFORCER: an event whose PRESENTATION is reinforcing.

NEGATIVE REINFORCER: an event whose TERMINATION is reinforcing.

AVERSIVE CONSEQUENCE: a "negative reinforcer" or a "punisher." It is sometimes convenient to use the more general term, "aversive consequence," because almost all "negative reinforcers" will usually also act as "punishers." However, sometimes an event may be a "punisher" but not a "negative reinforcer" or vice versa; so watch out.

REINFORCEMENT: the act of presenting a "reinforcer." "Reinforcer" is the event; "reinforcement" is the delivery of that event. An example: every time your parrot makes an obscene remark, you give it a cracker and are delighted to note the development of a foul-mouthed bird. The cracker is a "reinforcer." Giving the cracker to the bird contingent upon an obscenity is the act of "reinforcement." For this example to be meaningful it is helpful to assume that we are dealing with two dirty birds.

PUNISHMENT: the act of presenting a "punisher."

Reinforcers and punishers can also be categorized as to whether they are learned or unlearned.

CONSEQUATION: presentation of the consequences. "Consequation" is a general term which can refer to either "reinforcement" or "punishment." This term has been coined recently because it is frequently useful to talk about delivering the goods without specifying whether these goods are reinforcers or punishers. If you present a consequence following a response you would be said to CONSEQUATE that response.

UNCONDITIONED or PRIMARY REINFORCER: an event which does not require prior association with other reinforcers in order to have reinforcing properties. This is an unlearned reinforcer; its reinforcing value is biologically determined.

CONDITIONED or SECONDARY REINFORCER: an event which acquires its reinforcing properties through association with other reinforcers. This is a learned reinforcer.

UNCONDITIONED or PRIMARY PUNISHER and CONDITIONED or SECONDARY PUNISHER: I'll bet you can work this one out for yourself.

THE PREMACK PRINCIPLE: behavior which occurs frequently is more reinforcing than behavior which occurs less frequently. Therefore, the opportunity to engage in a high frequency behavior can be used as a reinforcer to increase the rate of lower frequency behaviors (recall how Behaviorman used this Principle in CON MAN Chapter 3. "If a kid prefers playing to reading, then you can use playing as a reinforcer for reading.").

CONTINGENCY: a sequential relation between two events. If one event occurs, the other will follow. We are concerned with several types of contingencies between behavior and its consequences.

POSITIVE REINFORCEMENT
CONTINGENCY: the behavior is followed by the PRESENTATION of a positive reinforcer.

NEGATIVE REINFORCEMENT or
ESCAPE CONTINGENCY: the behavior is followed by the termination of a negative reinforcer.

PUNISHMENT CONTINGENCY: the behavior is followed by the PRESENTATION of a punisher OR (now watch this, because it's tricky) the behavior is followed by the TERMINATION of a positive reinforcer. Examples: Due to your fantastic skill as a contingency manager, your parrot now has an active vocabulary that would make a sailer blush. (Even our rule "Nothing in Moderation" should probably be used in moderation.) Your wealthy and aging Aunt Minnie, Retired Admiral, U. S. Waves, will soon be visiting you. Since she is nautical but nice, your parrot will no doubt cause her to blush, be offended, and disinherit you. Oh, mercy, what to do? You can use a punishment contingency. Every time the bird says, "Hell," you can shake the hell out of it. This is the PRESENTATION of a punisher. Being the nonviolent type that you are, you might prefer the termination of a positive reinforcer. Every time the bird offends, you put the night cloth over his cage. That effectively terminates the positive reinforcer of the bird's being able to see you. You, of course, have no difficulty in assuming that your presence is a positive reinforcer for any man or beast.

AVOIDANCE CONTINGENCY: the behavior is followed by the prevention or postponement of a negative reinforcer (or punisher). This is the kind of contingency that Con Man implemented to help Johnathan Procrastinator write his thesis. If Johnathan completed a chapter of his dissertation within a month (the specified behavior), he would avoid losing $100 (postponement of the punisher).

DEADLINE CONTINGENCY: the reinforcing consequences (or postponement of aversive consequences) follow the specified behavior only if that behavior occurs within a specified period of time.

If the specified behavior occurs before the deadline is reached, the positive reinforcers will be presented (or the presentation of punishers will be avoided). If the specified behavior DOES NOT occur prior to the deadline, then there will be no positive reinforcers presented (in fact, punishers may be presented). Johnathan Procrastinator was also on a deadline contingency.

There is one final contingency. Maybe it shouldn't be classified as a contingency, since actually it is the absence of one. But here it is:

EXTINCTION PROCEDURE: withholding the reinforcement for a response that has been previously established through the use of that reinforcement.

If you use the extinction procedure, you will get

EXTINCTION BEHAVIOR: a reduction in the frequency of a response resulting from the extinction procedure. The response rate will gradually decrease until it is occurring no more frequently than prior to the use of reinforcement. When you use the term "extinction," it is a good idea to make it clear whether you are referring to the procedure or the behavior.

You are, no doubt, asking yourself, "What's the difference between the extinction procedure and the second type of punishment contingency, the one involving removal of positive reinforcement?" You weren't? Well, prepare yourself to learn more about these contingencies than you might care to know.

Consider your parrot. You were attempting to eliminate its swearing by terminating reinforcement every time it swore. Removal of the existing visual reinforcement for a period of time would be contingent upon its swearing. But that's a lot of work; you actually have to do something every time it makes the offending response; you have actively to take away a reinforcer.

But there's a much simpler procedure, the lazy man's procedure – "extinction". You don't have to take something away; just don't give it to him. The reason the bird went astray in the first place was that you laid a reinforcing cracker on it every time it swore. Stop reinforcing that bad behavior and it will extinguish.

The second type of punishment procedure is the withdrawal of an already present reinforcer CONTINGENT upon the occurence of the undesirable response. The extinction procedure is easier: simply stop the reinforcement contingency that was responsible for developing the response in the first place.

Of course, corrupting the morals of a bird is not as easy as we implied. If you had merely sat there, cracker in hand, waiting for that pure, innocent, untainted bird to gross you out, you would still be there. It is unlikely that it would have such a complex response in its repertoire. You had to use a complicated procedure called

THE METHOD OF SUCCESSIVE APPROXIMATION, or SHAPING: a method of differentially reinforcing responses which successively approximate the terminal response. At first, you reinforce any response which even vaguely resembles the desired response. After that crude first approximation is occurring with regularity, you require that the response be a little closer to what you're really after before you reinforce. You gradually stipulate that the response be more and more like the desired terminal response before you reinforce. You require that the response successively approximate the desired response; you require that the response get closer and closer to the form of the desired response. You use the "method of successive approximation." You SHAPE the response. You shouldn't expect your bird to say "hell" right off; so at first, you reinforce almost any kind of squawk. Eventually one squawk will sound a little more like "hell" than any of the others, and you reinforce. Then you wait until another response comes along that was at least that good before you deliver the goods. Gradually you

require that the squawk more and more closely approximate "hell" before you reinforce it.

Suppose you wish to teach the Limerick about the young lady from, etc................
You would be attempting to establish a

STIMULUS-RESPONSE CHAIN: a sequence of alternating stimuli and responses. Each response produces a stimulus which, in turn, causes the next response to occur. (This is not a very technical definition, but it will do for now.) If your bird learned his lesson well, each word he says will act as a stimulus for him to say the next word in the Limerick.

CONCURRENT SCHEDULE OF REINFORCEMENT: two or more sets of response-reinforcement contingencies are in effect concurrently. By "concurrent" we mean "at the same time." An example: a little old lady is attempting to cross the street at a busy intersection. Your response of helping her would be reinforced by her social approval, a "thank you," and you might even get a merit badge. On the other hand, your response of standing on the corner and watching her vainly attempt to avoid the onrush of traffic might be reinforced by the opportunity for a good laugh. That is an example of a situation where two incompatible responses are under the control of different reinforcement contingencies. In other cases, a single response might be under the control of two or more concurrently acting contingencies of reinforcement. The reason we mention the notion of "concurrent schedules of reinforcement" is to emphasize the point that to properly analyze most behavioral interactions you must look at more than one class of responses and more than one source of reinforcement.

PRINCIPLES: the following principles or behavioral laws are also relevant to this chapter.

THE BIRTH OF A CONDITIONED REINFORCER: a neutral event or consequence can become a reinforcer by being associated with a reinforcing consequence. This is not much more than a restatement of the definition of conditioned reinforcement, but it's so important that it's worth repeating.

An example: the only time the baby is ever fed, burped, diapered, coddled, or helped is when someone is paying attention to him. If no-one is in the room or paying attention to the baby, then very few unconditioned reinforcers — such as food and milk — will come its way.

The delivery of these reinforcing consequences is always associated with the attention of another human being. This attention is originally a neutral consequence, but due to continued association with various primary reinforcers, attention becomes a very powerful conditioned reinforcer. And this continues throughout life. Man is a social animal; it happens that many of his reinforcers are presented by other human beings. This leads to a related principle of behavior.

Social approval is one "hell" of a powerful conditioned reinforcer, at least for human beings. (I'm not too sure about hermit crabs.) Approval, attention, recognition, and praise are all lumped under one general category called SOCIAL REINFORCEMENT. And social reinforcement is what makes the world go around. But the importance of social reinforcement is very difficult to recognize because it is frequently quite subtle and hard to detect. The mere fact that someone will pay enough attention to you to listen while you talk is fantastically reinforcing. You develop all sorts of clever little conversational routines that are reinforced by the fact that they hold other people's attention. And if you can say something that will get laughs, that's dynamite. An important point to keep in mind is that we are usually unaware that our behavior is being influenced by these social reinforcers. You don't say to yourself, "I'm going to state something interesting, funny, and profound in order to latch on to a little social reinforcement from this guy." It's just that for some mysterious reason you say things that people will listen to. And the mysterious reason is that behavior which is reinforced will be more likely to occur again in the future. "Social reinforcement" is very heavy, so we'll pick up on it again later on.

Life is a bowl full of concurrent schedules, and your past history of reinforcement is an important influence in determining which response you make. If you've had a history of frequent reinforcement for helping people when they're in trouble, you'll probably help the little old lady across the street. But if you've had a history of frequent reinforcement for observing the Laurel and Hardy slapstick nature of man's inept attempts to deal with the world, you might watch her flounder. On the other hand, you may have neither history of reinforcement. In fact, the last time you intervened to lend a helping hand was when that big bully was beating up on the helpless lady (you, of course, on the side of the oppressed minority). Then the woman (no longer a lady) started beating on you because you had hurt her husband. Your good-Samaritan behavior was punished. So when you see the little old lady in trouble, what do you do? Eyes straight ahead and just keep right on truckin'.

"Gee, officer, I didn't even see the little old lady. If I'd known she was in trouble, you can be sure I'd of helped 'er. I feel just as bad about it as you do."

One more time: your past history of reinforcement is an important influence in determining which response you will make in a concurrent schedule of reinforcement.

OBJECTIVES

1. A behavioral consequence is:
   a) a relation between two events.
   b) a method of differentially reinforcing responses which successively approximate the terminal response.
   c) the result or consequence of the response or behavior.
   d) the relation between the behavior and the consequence.
   e) a & d.

2. The three basic types of behavioral consequences are (select three choices):
   a) reinforcing consequences
   b) extinction consequences
   c) neutral consequences
   d) deadline consequences
   e) punishing consequences

3. A reinforcer is:
   a) an event that increases the frequency of the behavior it follows.
   b) an event that decreases the frequency of the behavior it follows.
   c) a reinforcing consequence.
   d) an event that has no effect on the frequency of the behavior it follows.
   e) a & c.

4. A punisher is:
   a) an event that increases the frequency of the behavior it follows.
   b) an event that decreases the frequency of the behavior it follows.
   c) an event that has no effect on the frequency of the behavior it follows.
   d) a punishing consequence.
   e) b & d.

5. The two types of reinforcers are (select two choices):
   a) positive reinforcers.
   b) punishing reinforcers.
   c) negative reinforcers.
   d) neutral reinforcers.
   e) extinction reinforcers.

6. Which of the following results in an increase in the frequency of the behavior it follows?
   a) a neutral consequence
   b) a punisher
   c) a positive reinforcer
   d) a negative reinforcer
   e) c & d

7. A negative reinforcer is:
   a) an event whose presentation is reinforcing.
   b) an event whose termination is reinforcing.
   c) an event whose termination results in an increase in the frequency of the behavior it follows.
   d) an event whose termination results in a decrease in the frequency of the behavior it follows.
   e) b & c.

8. A punisher is defined as:
   a) an event that increases the frequency of the behavior it follows.
   b) an event which decreases the frequency of the behavior it follows.
   c) a person who does the punishing.
   d) the results or consequences of the behavior.
   e) none of the above.

9. Consequation is:
   a) a general term which can refer to either reinforcement or punishment.
   b) the presentation of the consequences.
   c) a sequential relation between two events.
   d) the behavior which is being strengthened.
   e) a & b.

10. An unconditioned reinforcer is:
    a) an event that does not require prior association with other reinforcers in order to have reinforcing properties.
    b) an event which acquires its reinforcing properties through association with other reinforcers.
    c) the same as a primary reinforcer.
    d) the same as a secondary reinforcer.
    e) a & c.

11. A conditioned reinforcer is:
    a) an event that does not require prior association with other reinforcers.
    b) an event which acquires its reinforcing properties through association with other reinforcers.
    c) the same as a primary reinforcer.
    d) an unlearned reinforcer.
    e) b & c.

12. An unconditioned punisher is:
    a) the same as a primary punisher.
    b) the same as a secondary punisher.
    c) an event whose termination is punishing.
    d) an event that does not require prior association with other punishers in order to have punishing properties.
    e) a & d.

13. The Premack Principle:
    a) states that a behavior which occurs frequently is more reinforcing than a behavior which occurs less frequently.
    b) states that reinforcement must be delivered immediately following a response.
    c) was used by Behaviorman to help the "Rotten Kids" develop better reading behavior.
    d) b & d.
    e) a & c.

14. A contingency is:
    a) the reinforcer or punisher that follows a behavior.
    b) a small endocrine gland in the brain which gives man his free will.
    c) a sequential relation between two events.
    d) the specified behavior.
    e) the consequence that follows the specified behavior.

15. In a punishment contingency:
    a) the behavior is followed by the termination of a punisher.
    b) the behavior is followed by the termination of a positive reinforcer.
    c) the behavior is followed by the presentation of a punisher.
    d) the behavior is followed by the presentation of a positive reinforcer.
    e) b & c.

16. In an avoidance contingency:
    a) the specified behavior is followed by the presentation of an aversive consequence.
    b) the specified behavior is followed by the termination of an aversive consequence.
    c) the specified behavior is followed by the presentation of a positive reinforcer.
    d) the reinforcing consequences follow the behavior only if that behavior occurs within a specified period of time.
    e) the specified behavior is followed by the postponement or prevention of an aversive consequence.

17. If the reinforcing consequences follow the specified behavior only if that behavior occurs within a specified period of time, then the contingency in effect is a:
    a) reinforcement contingency.
    b) extinction contingency.
    c) negative reinforcement contingency.
    d) deadline contingency.
    e) time-sharing contingency.

18. WITHHOLDING the reinforcement that has been maintaining a response is the definition of:
    a) negative reinforcement.
    b) extinction procedure.
    c) extinction behavior.
    d) punishment procedure.
    e) b & c.

19. In the extinction procedure, reinforcement is _____; in the second type of punishment contingency, reinforcement is _____ contingent upon a response.
    a) withheld
    b) presented
    c) contingent
    d) withdrawn
    e) delayed

20. The method of differentially reinforcing responses which successively approximate the terminal response is the definition of:
    a) the method of successive approximation.
    b) stimulus-response chaining.
    c) shaping.
    d) extinction behavior.
    e) a & c.

21. TRUE OR FALSE?
    A successive approximation is a unit of behavior (or a response).

22. TRUE OR FALSE?
    Shaping and the method of successive approximation are identical procedures (or methods) used to modify behavior.

23. TRUE OR FALSE?
    Shaping and a successive approximation are both the same.

24. A sequence of alternating stimuli and responses is called a:
    a) response pattern.
    b) stimulus trace.
    c) stimulus-response chain.
    d) concurrent schedule.
    e) a & b.

25. Which of the following are examples of social reinforcement? (Circle all of the correct choices.)
    a) attention
    b) food
    c) praise
    d) water
    e) money

26. TRUE OR FALSE?
    An individual's past history of reinforcement is of minor importance in determining his behavior.

ANSWERS

1. c; 2. a, d, e; 3. e; 4. e; 5. a & c; 6. e; 7. e; 8. b; 9. e; 10. e; 11. b; 12. e; 13. e; 14. c; 15. e; 16. e; 17. d; 18. b; 19. a & d (in that order); 20. e; 21. true; 22. true; 23. false; 24. c; 25. a & c; 26. false

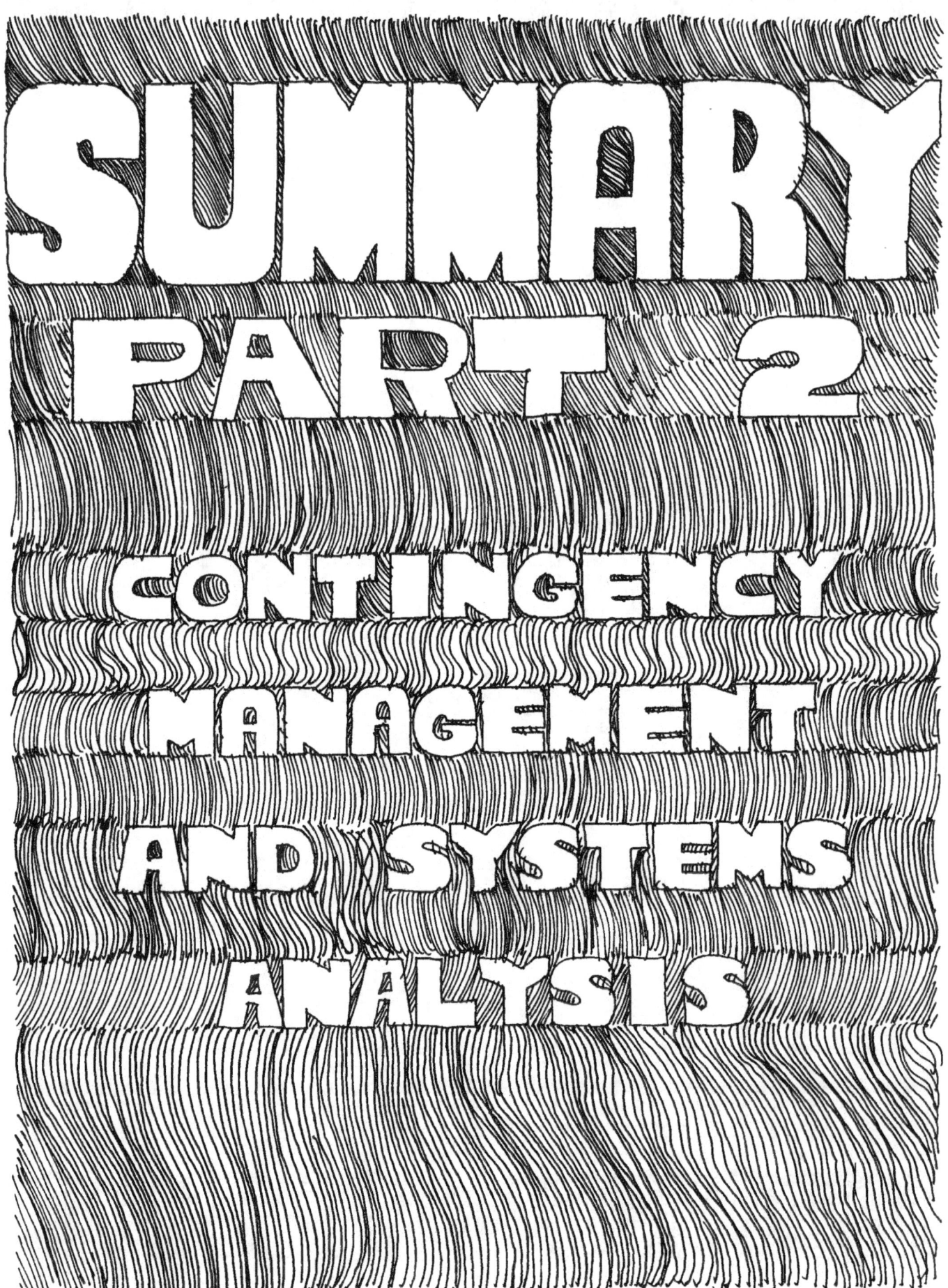

SUMMARY — PART 2 (CONTINGENCY MANAGEMENT AND SYSTEMS ANALYSIS)

THE THREE BASIC PHASES OF CONTINGENCY MANAGEMENT

OBSERVATION: it is necessary that you observe the behavior in order to deliver the consequences and in order to determine whether your contingency management program is working.

CONSEQUATION: after observing whether or not the behavior is occurring, you must deliver the reinforcing and/or punishing consequences according to your contingencies. Remember to be consistent in your consequation.

SPECIFICATION: specify the behaviors of interest, the consequences to be applied to that behavior, and the contingency between the behavior and the consequences.

THE RULES OF CONTINGENCY MANAGEMENT:

1. **NOTHING IN MODERATION (BE CONSISTENT)**: establish a reinforcement contingency and stick with it. It's easiest to be reasonable and make justifiable exceptions. The problem with being reasonable is that, almost always, the exceptions become more and more common, the behavior of the contingency manager gets more and more inconsistent, and the behavior being managed drifts farther and farther away from the objectives.

2. **THINK SMALL**: select very small and humble objectives for your behavioral system. If you do, you'll have at least a fighting chance of accomplishing something. But if your objective is to solve all the world's problems, you probably won't get anything accomplished. The world's problems will be solved by taking care of one little problem or objective at a time. There are two reasons you should select small behavioral objectives: first, you probably have only a limited amount of resources at your disposal. If you concentrate those limited resources on a small number of behavioral objectives, you will be more likely to develop a truly effective behavioral system. And second, the people whose behavior you are trying to modify have only a limited amount of time and energy to devote to your behavior modification system. If they concentrate their time and effort on a small number of behavioral objectives, they will be much more likely to accomplish something. The typical college is a good example of an ineffective behavior modification system. It could be considerably improved by thinking small and selecting a smaller set of behavioral objectives. Colleges have a limited amount of physical and personnel resources, yet they insist on having a wide variety of marginally effective programs. Instead, they should have a small number of programs that are clearly effective in helping students obtain their educational objectives. And they insist that students spread their limited time and effort very thinly over a wide variety of areas. The result is that the student is unable to accomplish many behavioral objectives that would have a lasting educational value after he left college.

3. **ESTABLISH FUNCTIONAL BEHAVIOR**: your objectives should specify behavior that will be reinforced in the real world once the behaver leaves the special contingency management system. If you don't establish functional behavior, the behavior will extinguish as soon as you turn your back. This is what students are asking for when they cry for "relevance." They want to achieve educational objectives that will result in behavior which will increase the effectiveness with which they deal with the real world. Behavior that is effective is behavior that is reinforced; and behavior that is reinforced does not extinguish, it stays with you.

4. **START WHERE THE BEHAVIOR IS AT**: when you specify an immediate behavioral objective, be sure that the behaver can accomplish it.
   Don't try to teach calculus to someone before he has learned algebra. Don't try to get someone to jump over a five-foot hurdle before he can jump over a three-foot hurdle.
   Most behavioral objectives make assumptions about what the behaver can already do. Frequently these assumptions are wrong.
   Just because a student is in the sixth grade does not mean he can read at the sixth grade level.
   So you've got to check and see if the behaver has the necessary prerequisite behaviors. If he doesn't, then you should specify some preliminary behavioral objectives that will help him get there.

5. **REINFORCE EACH UNIT OF A STIMULUS-RESPONSE CHAIN**: always divide large tasks into small steps and immediately reinforce the completion of each step. The problem with having one large reinforcer at the end of a long task is that the behavior may extinguish before the task is completed. If that big reinforcer in the sky is too far off, the behavior may not even get started. You'll find yourself procrastinating most on those big jobs that have very few reinforcers along the way but rely on a really heavy reinforcer at the end.

The large task that isn't broken down into small, reinforced steps has more going against it than extinction. It also has to compete against other activities that are being concurrently reinforced.

> Example: The large task — read 200 pages of a boring textbook, and at the end of the semester there will be a final exam offered as the big but distant reinforcer. A concurrently reinforced activity — watch "Laugh-In," and every 30 seconds something very funny and reinforcing will happen. You can bag the book.

Life is, indeed, a bowl full of concurrent schedules of reinforcement; if you understand that, you'll be in much better shape to deal effectively with life.

> More of the same example: use contingency management rule No. 5. Divide that large 200-page task into smaller steps — would you believe individual chapters? And the immediate reinforcer you provide could be the opportunity to take a brief quiz after each chapter. Studying may not compete effectively with "Laugh-In" still, but I bet it would beat "What's My Line?" Another way to sprinkle a few reinforcers along the way is to make the book interesting. An interesting book reinforces reading behavior. If we combined the immediate reinforcers of an interesting book and a quiz after each chapter, we might even wipe out "Laugh-In."

FIVE STEPS TO HEAVEN — OR — SYSTEMS ANALYSIS FOR THE PEOPLE*

SYSTEMS ANALYSIS: a way of getting the best job done most efficiently.

SYSTEM: people and things that affect each other.

*It really is five steps toward the heavens; because without systems analysis we probably wouldn't have gotten men on the moon. Ours is a considerably oversimplified, poor man's approach to systems analysis; but we are dealing with some of the essentials and hope that those readers who are more heavily into systems analysis will bear with us.

As a systems analyst, you'll be called on to look at a system and asked to figure out how to make it function better. Now we are primarily concerned with behavioral systems. That means we will try to help people interact better with each other and with their physical environment. We've said that there are five phases in systems analysis, but actually there is something you need to do before you begin phase 1. And it will be called:

PHASE 0 — a behavioral analysis: look at the behavioral system as it exists now and analyze it by using the concepts and principles of behavior you have come to know and love. What are the responses, what are the consequences, what are the contingencies, is extinction taking place where it should or shouldn't, is the method of successive approximation being used as necessary, are the stimulus-response chains being broken down into small, reinforced units, what's the story on concurrent schedules of reinforcement for competing behaviors, etc. Once you've done a behavioral analysis of the existing behavioral system, you are ready to begin the first phase of the actual systems analysis.

PHASE 1 — state the behavioral objectives: what sorts of behavior would you like to see in an improved behavioral system? Remember the second rule of contingency management — think small. Make sure your behavioral objectives are small enough that you'll actually be able to accomplish them.

> Example: the educational objectives of most colleges and most individual teachers are so grandiose that students would have to be geniuses to accomplish them. Since there are few genius types floating around, many teachers become disillusioned and bitter; they are sure that if they just had a few decent students they would be fantastic teachers.

> "But with today's generation of students, what can you do? Why should I bust a gut trying to help these kids if

they don't care themselves?"

Since the students are not achieving the teacher's unreasonable behavioral objectives, the teacher's teaching behavior is not getting reinforced. What happens to behavior that goes unreinforced? Right you are: to hell with it. Teaching is like sex: it's really reinforcing when it's going right, but if it's not, watch out. Teaching students who are not achieving their educational objectives may be more than just an extinction procedure; it may actually be aversive. Some teachers manage to escape into more reinforcing activities such as administration, research, committee meetings, and playing golf.

There is another cop-out left, however. A teacher can be very vague and general about his educational objectives. He can specify his educational objectives in non-behavioral terms so that it will be impossible to tell whether they are being accomplished.

"What I want is to develop the whole man; I want to help students find themselves."

That's cool, but if the teacher leaves it at that, no one will ever know how successful he is. However, there is more to it than that:

We must specify educational objectives in terms that involve OBSERVABLE BEHAVIOR. If we don't, we won't be able to apply the second and third phases of our contingency management procedure. Remember? Phase two — observe the behavior. And — phase three — consequate the behavior. If our educational objectives are not specified in terms of observable behavior, then forget it.

We should also keep in mind contingency management rule 2: establish functional behavior. We should specify behavioral objectives that will help the individual interact more effectively with his world, objectives that will be functional in producing more reinforcers for the individual. When you're thinking about reinforcers which the behavior will produce, remember that there is a lot more to the world than dollars and cents; a little coin never hurt anyone, but don't overlook more subtle reinforcers like social approval, etc.

Three major criteria for good behavioral objectives are that they should be:
1. attainable — think small
2. observable, and
3. functional.

PHASE 2 — design the behavioral system: draw on your vast storehouse of knowledge of behavioral principles and concepts to design a behavioral system that will accomplish the objectives you have stated. The fact that you did a thorough and insightful behavioral analysis of the existing system will be of considerable help in designing an improved system. If you know the concepts and principles currently operating, it will be much easier to modify the system to generate the kind of behavior you want.

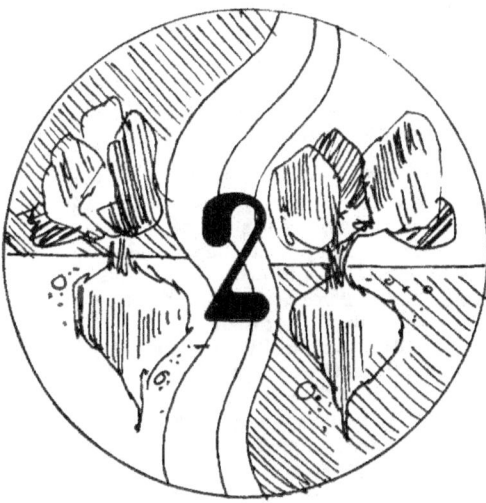

The design of a behavioral system involves the first phase of the general contingency management procedure: specification of the behavior, consequences, and contingencies involved. In specifying the behavior you will be working with, keep in mind contingency management rule 4: start where the behavior is at. If the individuals can't do what is initially expected of them, then you won't even be able to get started. Also remember contingency management rule 5: reinforce each unit of a stimulus-response chain. This is probably one of the reasons the original behavior system went wrong: there was too much reliance on the big reinforcer in the future. So be sure to specify each response or unit in the stimulus-response chain.

Next you need to specify the consequences. Use everything you can get your hands on -- positive reinforcers, negative reinforcers, punishers, unconditioned reinforcers (would you believe food), and opportunities for various activities. Don't forget the Premack Principle. This is a hotly debated point, but it has been our experience that it is almost impossible to design a complex behavioral system using only positive reinforcers; most systems also need a few aversive consequences to keep them going. Just try to keep the aversive consequences to a minimum and keep those positive reinforcers flowing fast and furiously.

Finally, you specify the contingencies — the relationships between the behavior and its consequences. In practice, of course, you will be considering the contingencies at the same time you select the consequences. Once again, most complex behavioral systems involve more than one type of contingency. Some of these contingencies and consequences will occur naturally, and you won't have to be responsible for insuring that they're in operation.

For example, if you are trying to teach a child to walk, you don't have to worry about teaching him not to run into walls and not to stand up under low tables; the punishment procedure established by the child's normal environment usually does an adequate job along these lines.

If all of the contingencies and consequences in the normal environment were adequate to maintain the behavioral system, then you wouldn't be called upon in the first place. So your job is to supplement the natural contingencies and consequences with some well-chosen ones of your own.

If the child is physically handicapped, it may well be the case that the normal environment will be inadequate to teach the child to walk. Your job would be to design a better environment, both human and physical, that would provide more effective contingencies and consequences.

Once again, keep in mind contingency management rule 5: reinforce each unit of a stimulus-response chain. We said that each unit should be specified, and, of course, a reinforcement contingency should also be attached to each of these units.

Don't expect a physically handicapped child to go through two hours of strenuous exercise every day unless you program a high density of reinforcement to maintain that behavior.

PHASE 3 -- implement the system: don't just talk about it, do it. Put your behavioral system into operation. If possible, you should first explain the design of the behavioral system to everyone involved. You should specify to the participants, as clearly as possible, the behavior, consequences, and contingencies. Where feasible, you should at least get their tentative consent to participate in the system.

Then you swing into the next two phases of the contingency management procedure: you observe the behavior and you consequate the behavior. And, of course, you always follow the third rule of contingency management — nothing in moderation. You consistently observe all the behavior that is specified in your design and you deliver the consequence exactly according to the contingencies specified in your design; you never moderate the contingencies or the consequences. Never make an exception; never change contingencies in the middle of the stream. If someone comes up with a plausible exception to your procedure, stick to your guns, but make a note of that exception for the final phase of our systems design. That way you will have a behavioral system that is flexible but not wishy-washy.

PHASE 4 -- evaluate the system: be empirical; actually measure the extent to which your system is accomplishing its objectives. Most behavioral systems are never evaluated in terms of the accomplishment of their original objectives.

For example, most colleges and universities have no notion of whether or not they are accomplishing their behavioral objectives. As a result, millions of dollars and millions of man-hours are probably being wasted every year in higher education. And colleges and universities are typical of most behavioral systems.

There are at least three levels at which you can evaluate your system:

1. Evaluation of the procedure: you've specified the consequences and contingencies, but are they actually being applied consistently? Is your system really being implemented? The only way you can be sure is to actually look and measure the performance of the participants. It will usually not be enough to simply ask them whether the contingencies and consequences are being used consistently as specified in your original design.

A grade-school teacher may really think

that she is following the specifications of the system, but when you actually watch her and record data on her performance, you may find that she is inadvertently reinforcing undesirable behavior and extinguishing good study behavior.

In our "Introduction to Psychology" course, it is necessary to be certain that the student teaching apprentices are correctly informing the students, that they are correctly administering and grading the quizzes, etc.

If your behavioral system is very complex, it may take quite a while before you have gotten all of the bugs out of the procedures; but you should make sure that the intended contingencies and consequences are in effect before you go on to the next level of evaluation.

2. Evaluation of the specific behaviors: in the design, you specified certain behaviors or responses you wished to deal with. Are the contingencies and consequences having the intended effect on those behaviors; have you gotten a sufficiently high rate of occurrence of the desirable behaviors and a sufficiently low rate of the undesirable behaviors?

For example: in our "Introduction to Psychology" course, the students should be attending class regularly and doing well on their daily quizzes.

You should make sure that the specific behaviors are occurring at the desired rates before going on to the final level of evaluation.

3. Evaluation of the performance of the overall behavioral objectives: once you know the procedures are being carried out properly and that the specific behaviors are occurring at the desired rates, you can then test the overall effectiveness of the system. Are the overall behavioral objectives being accomplished?

For our "Introduction to Psychology" course, we cannot be content just to evaluate the daily performance of our teaching apprentices and students; we must also be concerned with the overall outcome of the course. One of the outcomes is the students' terminal performance on a cumulative final exam.

It should be recognized that most complex systems have a whole set of behavioral objectives, and that sometimes increasing the degree of accomplishment of one objective hinders the accomplishment of other objectives.
The multiple objectives of our psychology course include a high rate of student mastery of the principles of behavior, a high rate of student mastery of the technology of contingency management, a high evaluation of the course by the students, and a high rate of enrolling in subsequent psychology courses. An ultimate objective also includes a high rate of usage of the content of this course, even after the students have completed the course. Not only are there overall objectives for the students' participation in the course, but there are also terminal objectives for the other participants, the teaching apprentices, the assistants, and the faculty. When specifying the terminal objectives of a system, you should consider all the participants.

PHASE 5 — recycle through the phases of systems analysis: if your overall behavioral objectives are not being accomplished, then you need to start all over; any new behavioral system with much complexity will never achieve its overall objectives during its first evaluation. You may want to reconsider your behavioral analysis of phase zero. Perhaps you incorrectly identified some of the reinforcers and punishers operating in the traditional system. For example, you might have assumed that the opportunity to listen to a professor giving a lecture would be an effective reinforcer for maintaining a high rate of textbook reading on the part of the students. This assumption is generally false.

You may have only to go back as far as phase one and reexamine your behavioral objectives. It will usually be the case that you didn't think small enough. Given the amount of resources you have and the amount of time the participants have, it may not be possible to accomplish all of the behavioral objectives you initially specified.

You may have anticipated that your students could master 500 complex concepts and read 1,000 pages in a one-semester course. This may be more than twice what is realistic, and after suffering a severe disappointment, you and your students now realize this.

Almost always you will need to repeat phase 2 and redesign your system, i. e., go back to the drawing board. Often it will be apparent that the behavioral system is not functioning properly in several areas, and that only the greatest of luck would allow the ultimate objectives to be accomplished.

> A closer inspection of the textbooks we use in college courses frequently shows that they do not adequately prepare the students to answer the questions on the quizzes we give them. We will have to change or supplement the texts or change the quiz questions.

It is at this point that you may want to consider seriously any suggestions made by the participants in the system. Frequently their involvement will allow them to be quite insightful. If the participants have some familiarity with the principles of behavior, contingency management, and systems analysis, their suggestions will be much more likely to be helpful.

> In our college courses, we find that the students' failure to complain about anything will not necessarily mean that all the procedures are being carried out properly; however, if several students complain about the same thing, then it is a serious candidate for readjustment.

After you have come up with a new design for your behavioral system, it is time to go into phase 3 — re-implement the system. If at first you don't succeed, etc.

> With our college courses, we have found that it is very wise to avoid implementing a new system in the middle of the semester. Even though you see several ways to improve the system, most participants find such mid-stream changes very aversive and complain about the poor organization of the course.

Now you proceed into phase 4 and evaluate your new system. Hopefully it will be a little better than the last time, but there will probably still be room for improvement. You young whippersnappers should remember this famous old saying: "Complex behavioral systems were never built in a day." And anyone who tells you how simple it is to build a better world is probably selling something besides the truth.

> Each semester we evaluate our psychology course and find there is considerable room for improvement. For example, less than 90% of the students achieve "A" level mastery of the course content, but we are gradually getting there.

Now you keep a stiff upper lip and prepare for the final phase — you recycle once again.

> Each semester we recycle our courses through the phases of systems analysis in order to get them closer to achieving our ultimate objectives.

OBJECTIVES

1. The three basic phases of contingency management are (select three choices):
   a) recyclization
   b) consequation
   c) continuation
   d) observation
   e) specification

2. Which one of the following is not a rule of contingency management?
   a) Nothing in moderation
   b) Think small
   c) Establish functional behavior
   d) Start where you think the behavior should be
   e) Reinforce each unit of a stimulus-response chain

3. Dividing large tasks into small steps and immediately reinforcing the completion of each step exemplifies which rule of contingency management?
   a) Nothing in moderation
   b) Think small
   c) Start where you think the behavior should be
   d) Reinforce each unit of a stimulus-response chain
   e) Be consistent

4. Selecting very small and humble objectives for a behavioral system exemplifies which rule of contingency management?
   a) Be consistent
   b) Reinforce each unit of a stimulus-response chain
   c) Think small
   d) Be objective
   e) Nothing in moderation

5. The typical college is a good example of an ineffective behavior modification system because:
   a) the student-faculty ratio is too high.
   b) effective behavior modification is too expensive.
   c) the college's objectives are too large and varied.
   d) students' behavior is almost impossible to modify.
   e) none of the above.

6. The large task that isn't broken down into small reinforced steps may never be completed because of:
   a) lack of time and energy.
   b) extinction.
   c) other competing behaviors being concurrently reinforced.
   d) lack of ability.
   e) b & c.

7. Systems analysis is:
   a) people and things that affect each other.
   b) another way of saying reinforcement contingency.
   c) the first rule of contingency management.
   d) a way of getting the best job done most efficiently.
   e) all of the above.

8. TRUE OR FALSE?
   A system is people and things that affect each other.

9. Before starting Phase 1 of systems analysis, you must:
   a) design a better behavioral system than the one that currently exists.
   b) state the behavioral objectives of your new system.
   c) look at the behavioral system as it now exists and analyze it is terms of behavioral principles and concepts.
   d) recycle your new behavioral system through the phases of systems analysis.
   e) b & d.

10. In Phase 1 of systems analysis (stating the behavioral objectives), one should:
    a) do everything in moderation.
    b) think small.
    c) attempt to establish functional behavior.
    d) design a new behavioral system.
    e) b & d.

11. In designing the new behavioral system, one should:
    a) specify the behavior.
    b) specify the consequences.
    c) specify the contingencies.
    d) all of the above.
    e) none of the above.

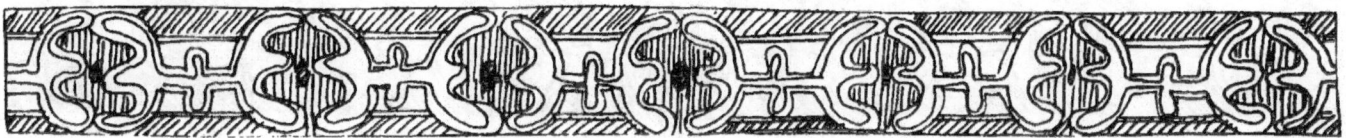

12. TRUE OR FALSE?
    Before implementing the new behavior system, it is desirable to specify the behavior, consequences, and contingencies to the participants.

13. After implementing the system it is important to consequate the behaviors:
    a) in moderation
    b) intermittently
    c) consistently
    d) severely
    e) subjectively

14. In evaluating the system, one should:
    (Circle all the correct choices.)
    a) evaluate the specific behaviors.
    b) evaluate the procedure.
    c) evaluate as subjectively as possible.
    d) evaluate the effectiveness of the overall behavioral objectives.
    e) recycle through the phases of systems analysis.

15. The final phase of systems analysis is to:
    a) evaluate the system.
    b) evaluate the procedure.
    c) recycle through the phases of systems analysis.
    d) terminate the system.
    e) state your behavioral objectives.

16. The three major criteria for good behavioral objectives are that they should be _____, _____, and _____
    a) time-consuming
    b) functional
    c) vague
    d) observable
    e) accomplishable

17. TRUE OR FALSE?
    Once you have gone through the six phases of systems analysis (phase 0 — phase 5), your behavioral system will run as efficiently as possible.

ANSWERS

1. b, d, e; 2. d; 3. d; 4. c; 5. c; 6. e; 7. d; 8. true; 9. c; 10. e; 11. d; 12. true; 13. e; 14. a, b, d; 15. c; 16. b, d, e; 17. false

NOW ME AN' MY OLD LADY HAVE JUST FINISHED A VERY HEAVY, OUTA-SIGHT DINNER. (SINCE WE'VE FINISHED IT, IT MUST BE OUTA-SIGHT.) WE'RE REALLY FULL, BUT WE'RE TRYING TO GET THE SWEETS' MONKEY OFF OUR BACKS, SO WE DON'T HAVE ANY DESSERT.

IT'S TIME TO GO TO THE FLICK.

...... AND **THIS** TIME WE'RE GONNA BE REALLY COOL — NO SNACKS!

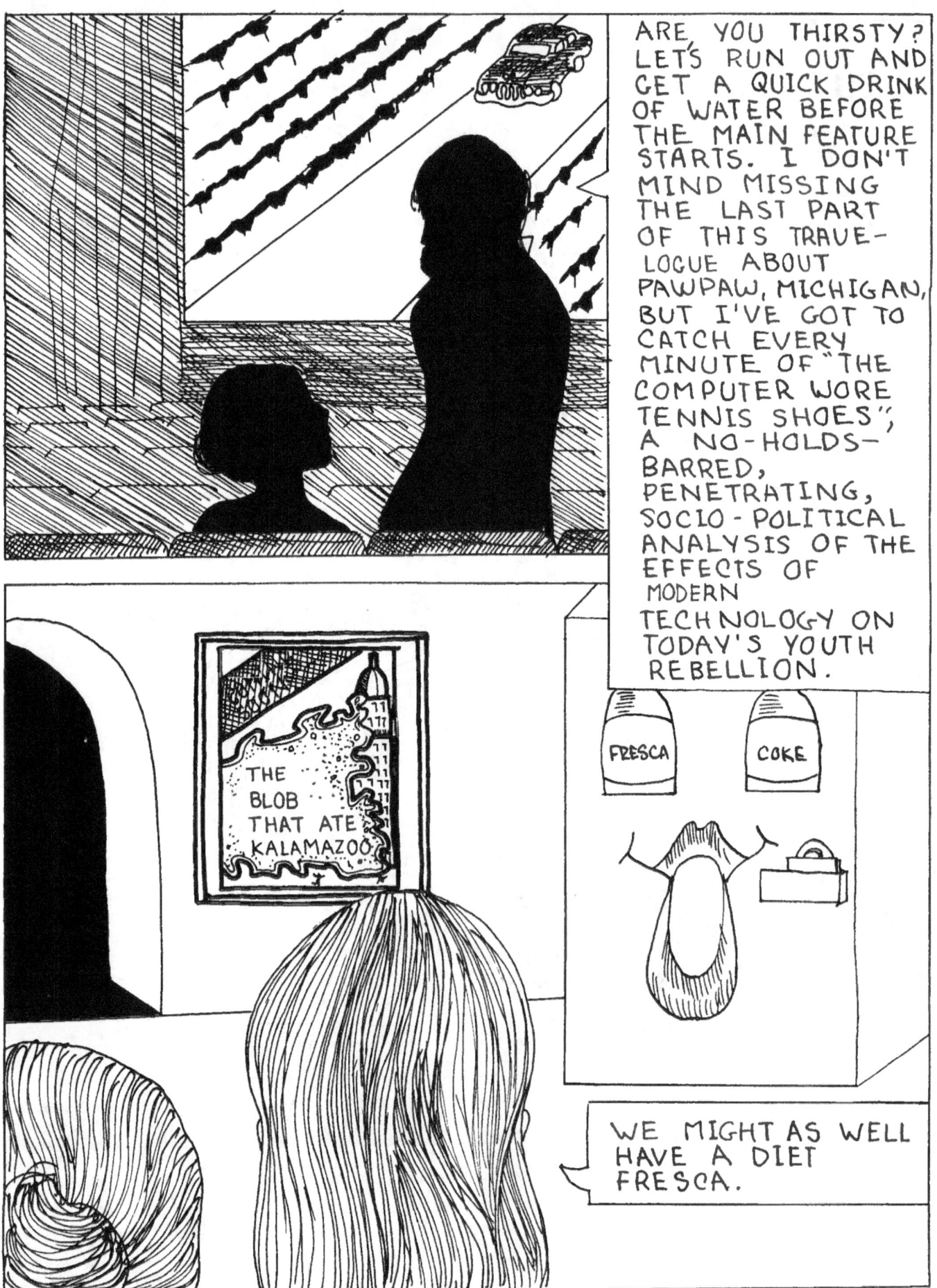

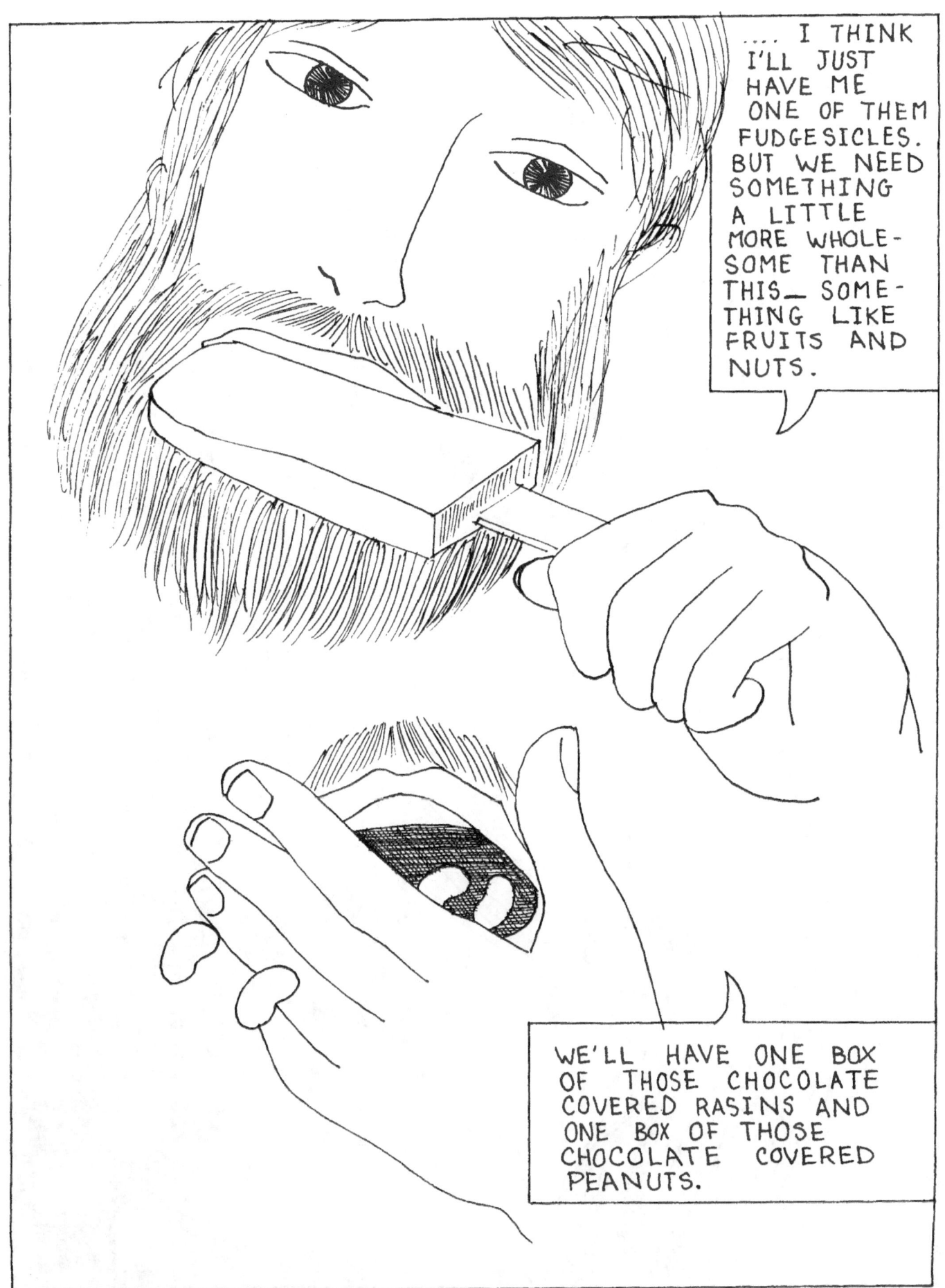

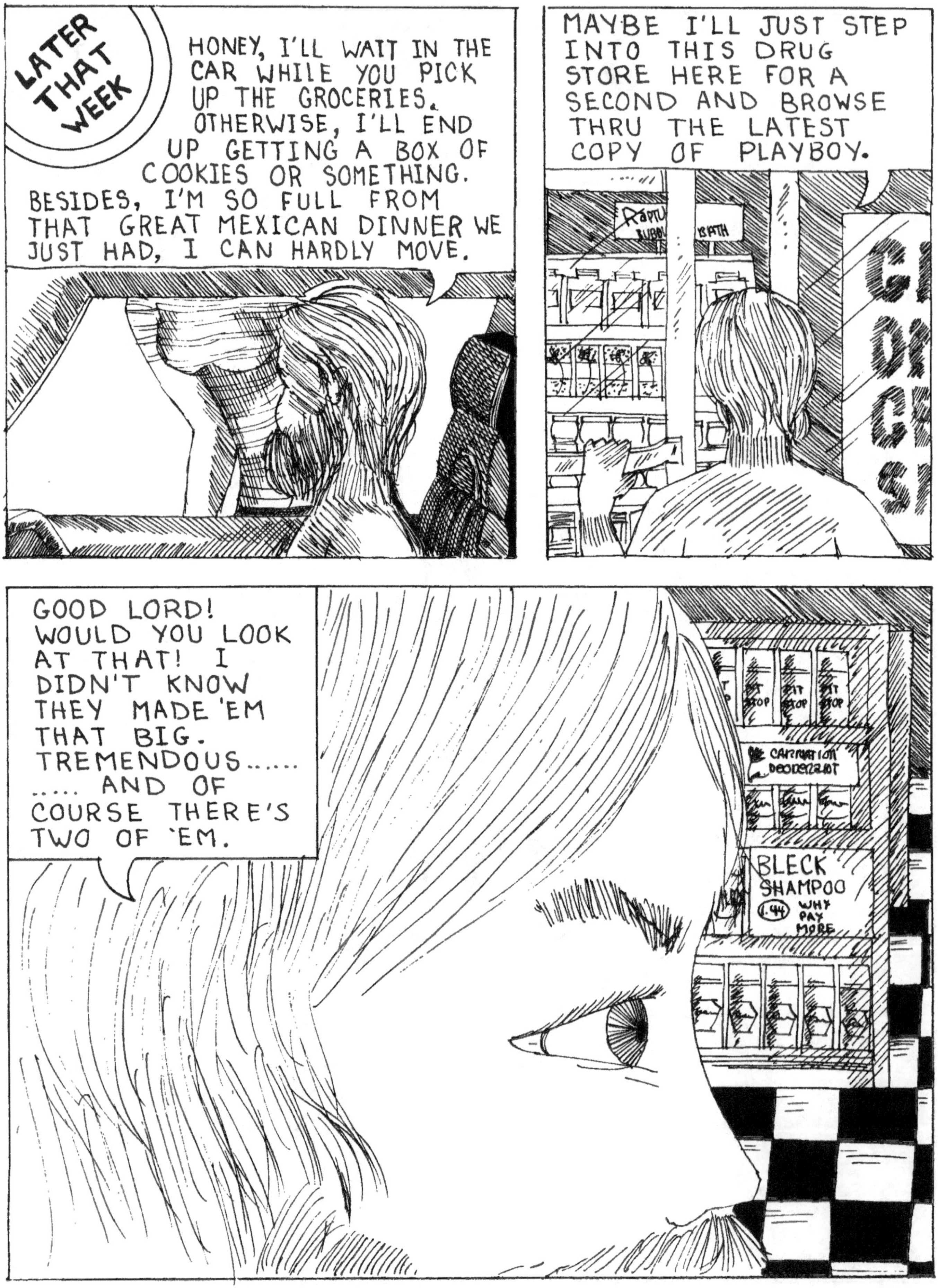

LATER THAT WEEK

"HONEY, I'LL WAIT IN THE CAR WHILE YOU PICK UP THE GROCERIES. OTHERWISE, I'LL END UP GETTING A BOX OF COOKIES OR SOMETHING. BESIDES, I'M SO FULL FROM THAT GREAT MEXICAN DINNER WE JUST HAD, I CAN HARDLY MOVE."

"MAYBE I'LL JUST STEP INTO THIS DRUG STORE HERE FOR A SECOND AND BROWSE THRU THE LATEST COPY OF PLAYBOY."

"GOOD LORD! WOULD YOU LOOK AT THAT! I DIDN'T KNOW THEY MADE 'EM THAT BIG. TREMENDOUS...... ..... AND OF COURSE THERE'S TWO OF 'EM."

7-7

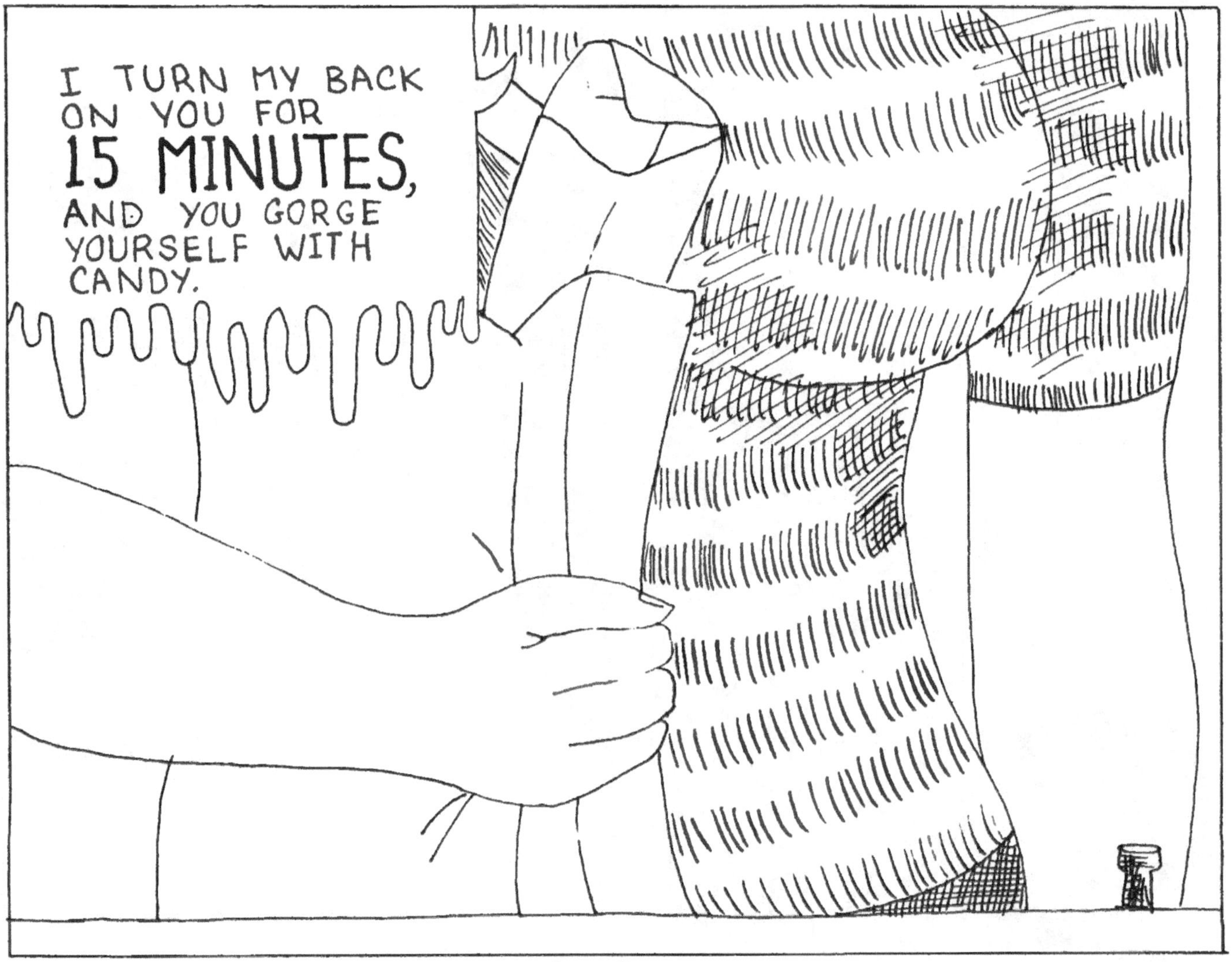

"I DON'T KNOW WHY, BUT I CAN'T RESIST SWEETS. EATING SWEETS IS JUST A HABIT!"

OVEREATING IS A COMMON PROBLEM, AND BEHAVIORAL SCIENCE IS NOT SURE WHAT THE CAUSE IS.

THERE ARE CERTAIN SITUATIONS WHERE FOOD IS A REINFORCER, ALTHOUGH THE PERSON IS CLEARLY NOT DEPRIVED OF FOOD.

WE JUST DON'T KNOW ENOUGH ABOUT THOSE SITUATIONS YET.

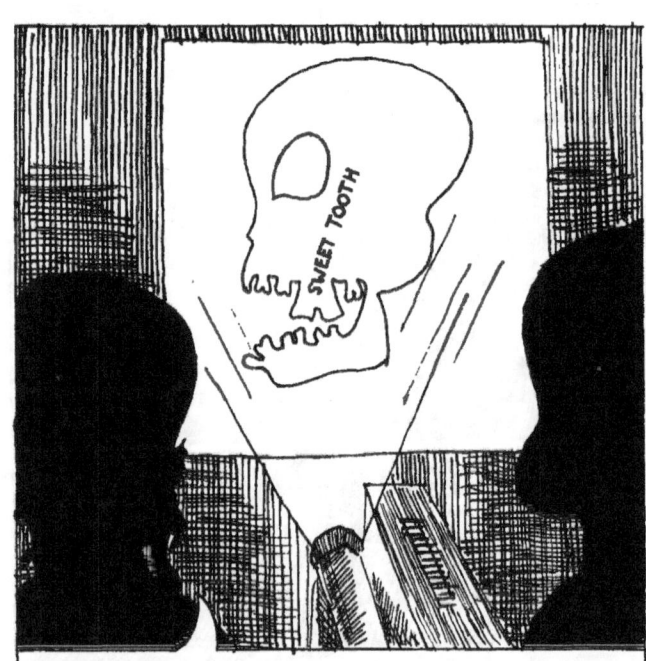

HOWEVER, WE DO KNOW HOW TO DEAL WITH THE PROBLEM. YOUR MAIN PROBLEM IS THAT YOUR "SWEET TOOTH" MAKES YOU OVEREAT, SO YOU'RE GETTING FAT.

"LET'S CONCENTRATE PRIMARILY ON YOUR WEIGHT."

"SOUNDS GOOD TO ME."

MAKE A GRAPH AND PLOT YOUR WEIGHT ON IT EACH MORNING. TRY TO CUT DOWN ON YOUR EATING SO THAT YOU LOSE AT LEAST ONE HALF POUND EACH DAY UNTIL YOU BECOME THAT FINE FIGURE OF A MAN WE ALL KNOW YOU REALLY ARE.

GOLLY, I'M NOT TOO SURE THAT'LL DO ANY GOOD.

IT MAY NOT, BUT IT'S WORTH A TRY. WATCHING THAT GRAPH DROP DOWN ONE HALF POUND EACH DAY MAY BE ENOUGH OF A **SECONDARY POSITIVE REINFORCER** TO KEEP YOU GOING.

I'M STILL SKEPTICAL.

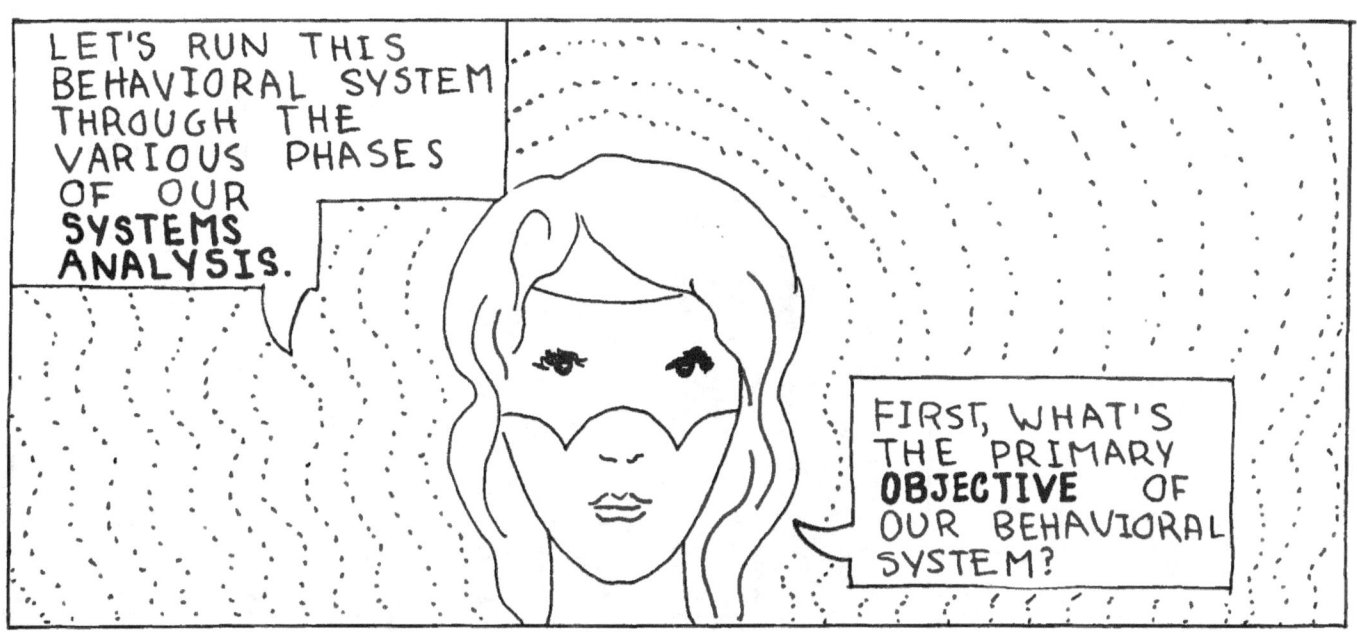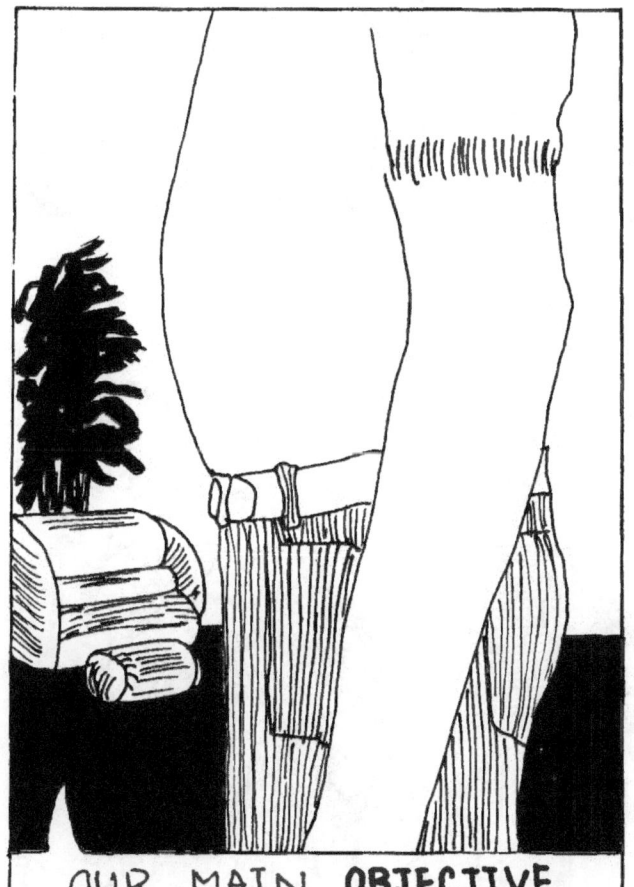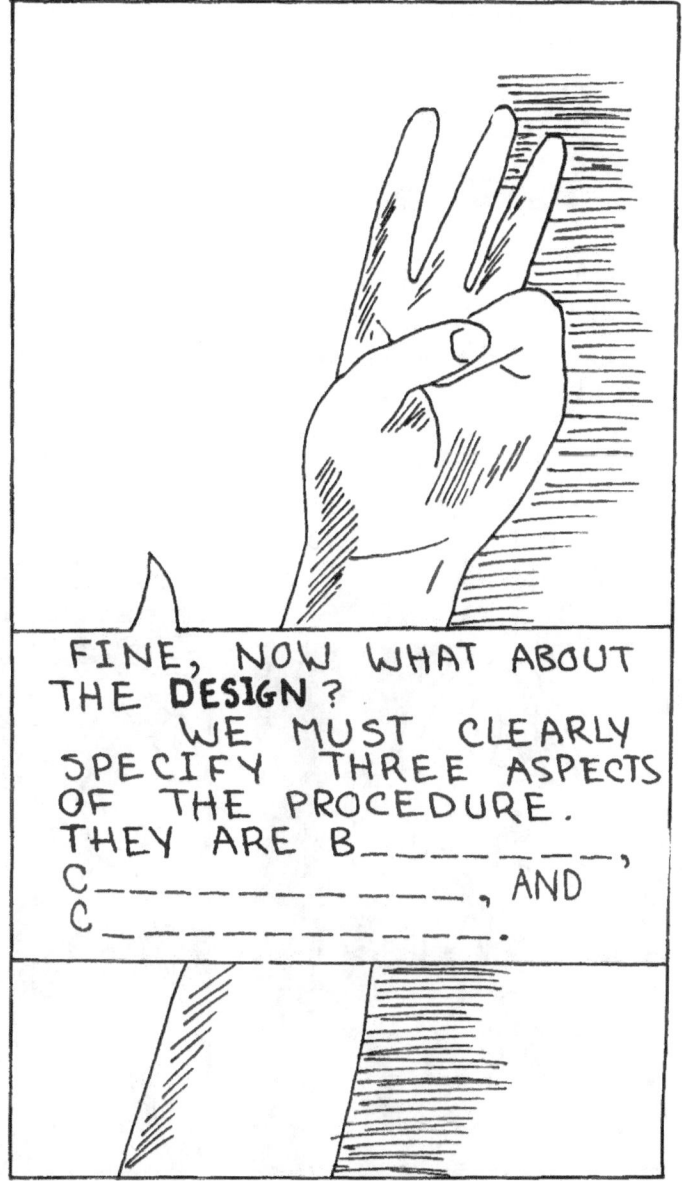

"WE RECYCLE; WE START AGAIN, ADDING AN AVOIDANCE CONTINGENCY. ALONG WITH AN ADDITIONAL CONSEQUENCE."

"YOU MEAN.... I HAVE TO LOSE A HALF A POUND A DAY IN ORDER TO AVOID HAVING SOME BAD THING HAPPEN TO ME?"

"RIGHT, AND HERE'S THE BADDIE: ANY DAY THAT YOU FAIL TO DROP A HALF A POUND, YOU HAVE TO CLEAN UP SEVENTY-FIVE PIGEON CAGES IN THE PSYCHOLOGY DEPARTMENT'S RESEARCH LABORATORY."

GASP

7-16

LET'S CHANGE THE **SPECIFIED BEHAVIOR** JUST A LITTLE BIT. WE'LL DRAW A LINE ON YOUR GRAPH THAT SHOWS WHAT YOUR WEIGHT SHOULD BE IF YOU DROP A HALF A POUND EACH DAY.

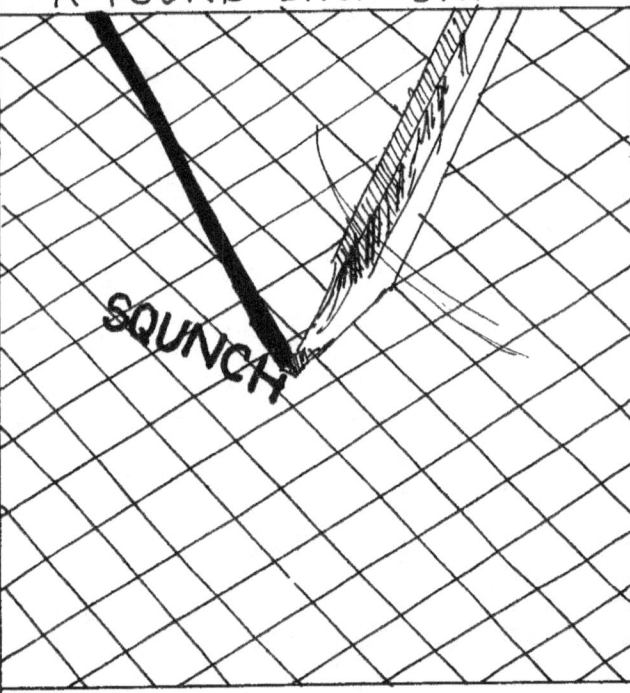

THAT WAY, IF YOU GET A POUND OR TWO AHEAD OF YOUR WEIGHT-REDUCTION SCHEDULE, YOU'VE GOT A LITTLE MARGIN OF SAFETY.

THE BEHAVIORAL REQUIREMENT WILL BE SIMPLY THAT YOU STAY AT OR BELOW THAT LINE. IF YOU DROP A COUPLE OF POUNDS ONE DAY, YOU WON'T HAVE TO DROP ANY THE NEXT DAY — JUST AS LONG AS YOU STAY BELOW THE CRITERION LINE.

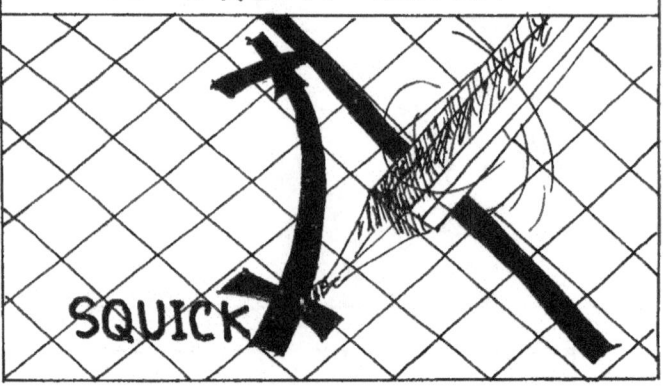

TWO DAYS LATER

HUMM..... I'M A QUARTER OF A POUND HEAVIER THAN I SHOULD BE. OH WELL, I'LL MAKE IT UP TOMORROW. THERE'S NO NEED TO CLEAN THE PIGEON CAGES FOR ONE QUARTER OF A POUND.

SEVERAL DAYS LATER

WELL, IN FIFTEEN DAYS I DROPPED SEVEN AND A HALF POUNDS. YOUR BEHAVIOR MODIFICATION SYSTEM REALLY WORKS. IT ELIMINATED MY OVEREATING, AND I ADOPTED A MUCH MORE SENSIBLE DIET. AS YOU EXPECTED, THE THING I DROPPED OUT FIRST WAS THE CANDY WITH ALL THOSE CALORIES.

AND NOW THAT HE'S BECOME SUCH A FINE FIGURE OF A MAN, I'M NO LONGER ASHAMED TO BE SEEN IN PUBLIC WITH HIM.

THERE'S NO HASSLE IN THE WHOLE THING. AS A MATTER OF FACT, I KIND OF DUG IT, BUT I'M AFRAID WE'RE GOING TO HAVE TO CONTINUE THIS PROCEDURE IF I'M TO MAINTAIN MY GOOD EATING BEHAVIOR AND KEEP MY WEIGHT DOWN TO 155 POUNDS.

WE COULD SIMPLY SAY THAT ANY TIME YOU EAT SO MUCH THAT YOU GO OVER 155 POUNDS, YOU HAVE TO CLEAN THE PIGEON CAGES, BUT I'D RATHER USE A SLIGHTLY LOOSER PROCEDURE. LET'S SAY THAT YOU GET WEIGHED EVERY DAY AND THAT ANY DAY THAT YOU GO OVER 155 POUNDS, WE HAVE TO START THE SAME OLD WEIGHT REDUCTION PROCEDURE WE'VE HAD. THAT WAY, IF YOU'RE UNDER 155 POUNDS AND YOU SPLURGE ONE DAY AND REALLY MAKE A PIG OF YOURSELF, IT'S NO BIG HASSLE.

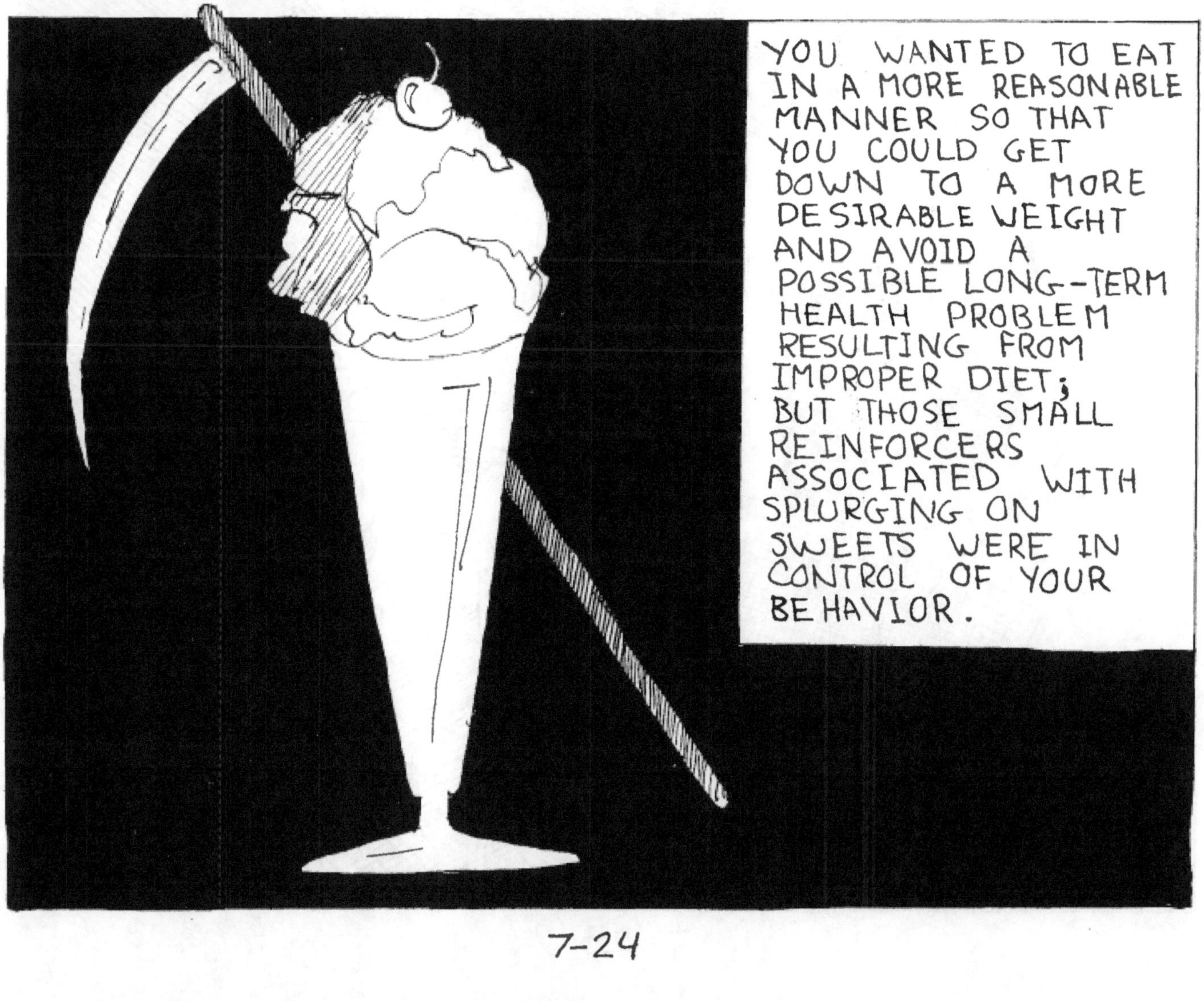

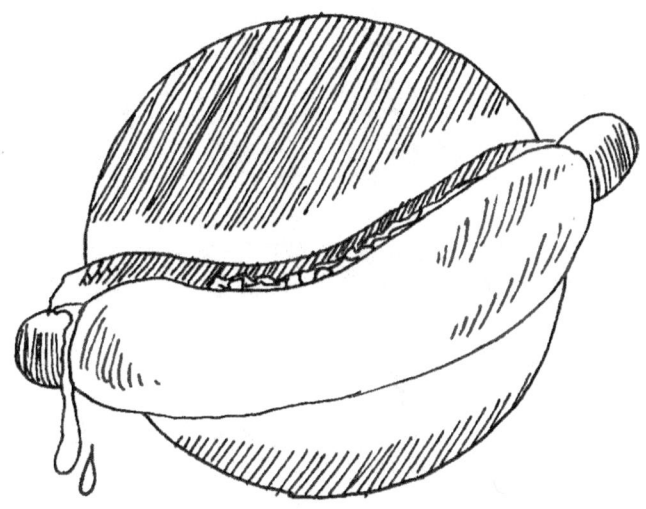

RECAP

1. It is not for an EMPIRICAL psychology to speculate about internal causes of problem behavior. That is why Behaviorwoman did not attempt to cure any internal cause of the Candy Fiend's overeating. Instead, she worked with weight change, which is observable behavior. Observable behavior is the ONLY indication of problems we have. Since "internal causes" are not observable, all we can do is speculate about their existence. The problem we start with IS the behavior, and once this behavior is changed, the problem no longer exists.

2. The preferred technique for contingency management is to apply consequences to the problem behavior itself, rather than to behavior that is assumed to cause the problem. Behaviorwoman initially consequated overeating. Overeating is apparently the cause of overweight; however, weight change itself should be the behavior consequated because it is the desired behavior. Thus overeating AND any other variables that contribute to weight gain are consequated when no weight decrease occurs.

3. It is usually the case that small, frequent reinforcers will be more effective in controlling behavior than more potent, but long-term reinforcers.

Dr. Malott:

Weight change is NOT behavior; it is an observable product of changed eating behavior that has reduced the person's caloric intake. It could also result from increased exercise. Skinner refers to your kind of procedure as "reinforcing an outcome," and he suggests that it is a poor way to build skill because it doesn't respect the topography of behavior. In THE TOKEN ECONOMY, Allyon and Azrin make the point that if you can't directly observe behavior, you arrange for the correct response to produce some enduring change in the environment upon which reinforcement can be made contingent. In any case, weight loss is NOT behavior.

R. Ludlow

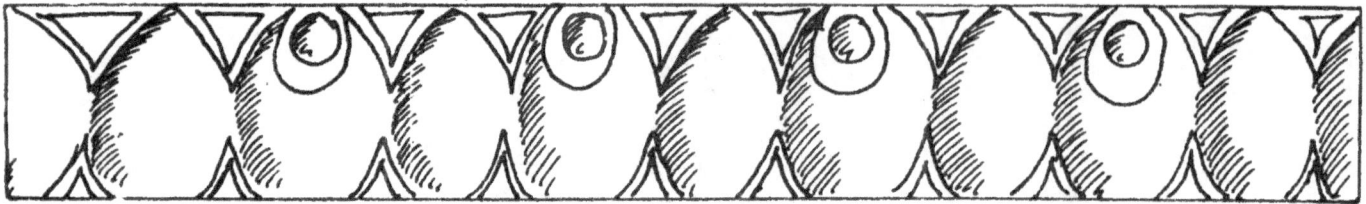

OBJECTIVES

1. For the problem of overeating, behavioral science would directly consequate
   a) the cause.
   b) weight.
   c) eating.
   d) the environment.
   e) all of the above.

2. PLEASE NOTE: objective 1 illustrates a very obvious, important point in contingency management which, unfortunately, is often overlooked. The behavior that you measure (and are trying to strengthen or weaken) must be the behavior you consequate. In objective 1, the desired behavior is weight loss. We don't care how much the individual eats or doesn't eat, as long as he loses weight. When weight gain is consequated, eating becomes its own consequence. Even Behaviorwoman made that mistake at first.

3. The phases of systems analysis are (Choose all that are correct):
   a) state the primary objective of the behavioral system.
   b) specify the behavior, contingency, and consequence.
   c) implement the procedure.
   d) test the procedure.
   e) change the procedure if it isn't working.

4. A lot of small, immediate reinforcers are _____ effective (as/than) long-term reinforcers of fairly high magnitude.
   a) more
   b) less
   c) equally

ANSWERS

1. b; 3. a, b, c, d, e; 4. a.

7 — 27

BEHAVIOR BAG

LETTERS FROM YOU TO US. YOU, TOO, CAN GET A LETTER PRINTED, BUT DON'T BET ON IT. SEND ALL LETTERS TO BEHAVIORDELIA, 474 ACADEMY, KALAMAZOO, MICH. 49007.

DEAR UNCLE DICKIE,
  IN CON MAN #144, P. 1-12, YOG-KNISH LEFT THE SCENE AND DIDN'T RETURN. WHERE DID HE GO? I AM A LOYAL FAN OF HIS, SO PLEASE SEND AN ANSWER.
            GARY R., PAWPAW.

DEAR GARY,
CHECK P. 1-31. THOUGH THE WINDOW OF THE SLUM APARTMENT OF JOHN + MARSHA YOU'LL SEE THE SOUTH WALL OF THE MOXIE BOTTLING PLANT. OLD YOG WAS MERELY HEADED OUT TO WORK ON THE CAP-STAMPER. HE WORKS THE 4-O-CLOCK SHIFT. EXPECT TO SEE YOG IN ACTION SOON, THOUGH.
            UNCLE DICKIE.

DEAR UNCLE DICKIE,
  I THINK I UNDERSTAND THE QUANTUM GAP, AT LAST. WHEN BEHAVIORMAN REMOVED THE FRILLIC GLOBE HE CAUSED A RIFT IN GONZOii'S POWER SPHERE, WHICH GENERALIZED TO A GAP IN THE ENTIRE QUANTUM UNIVERSE. TRUE OR INACCURATE?
        LESTER O'BERGMIER-OSHTEMO

DEAR LESS,
  NICE TRY, BUT NO CIGAR.
        UNCLE DICKIE.

DEAR UNCLE DICKIE,
  FOR SOME TIME I'VE BEEN BOTHERED BY UGLY WARTS AND ICHY SKIN ON MY NECK. WHAT DO YOU THINK?   ED.

I THINK YOU GOT THE WRONG COLUMN, DUMBO. UNCLE D.

I REALLY LIKE RALPH, BUT I CAN'T STAND WATCHING HIM RUN HIS FINGERS LOVINGLY THROUGH HIS BEARD!

YES, I STARTED OUT INNOCENTLY ENOUGH AS A BEARD FONDLER. NOT REALLY EXCESSIVE LIKE SOME MEN....

JUST AN OCCASIONAL STROKE. DIFFERENT STROKES FOR DIFFERENT FOLKS. MUCH TO MY ALARM, I DISCOVERED THAT THE LONGER MY BEARD GREW, THE MORE FREQUENT AND THE MORE ELABORATE MY BEARD FONDLING BECAME.

THEN I STARTED SOMETHING THAT WAS EVEN MORE DISGUSTING: I STARTED JERKING THE HAIRS OUT OF MY BEARD — ONE AT A TIME.

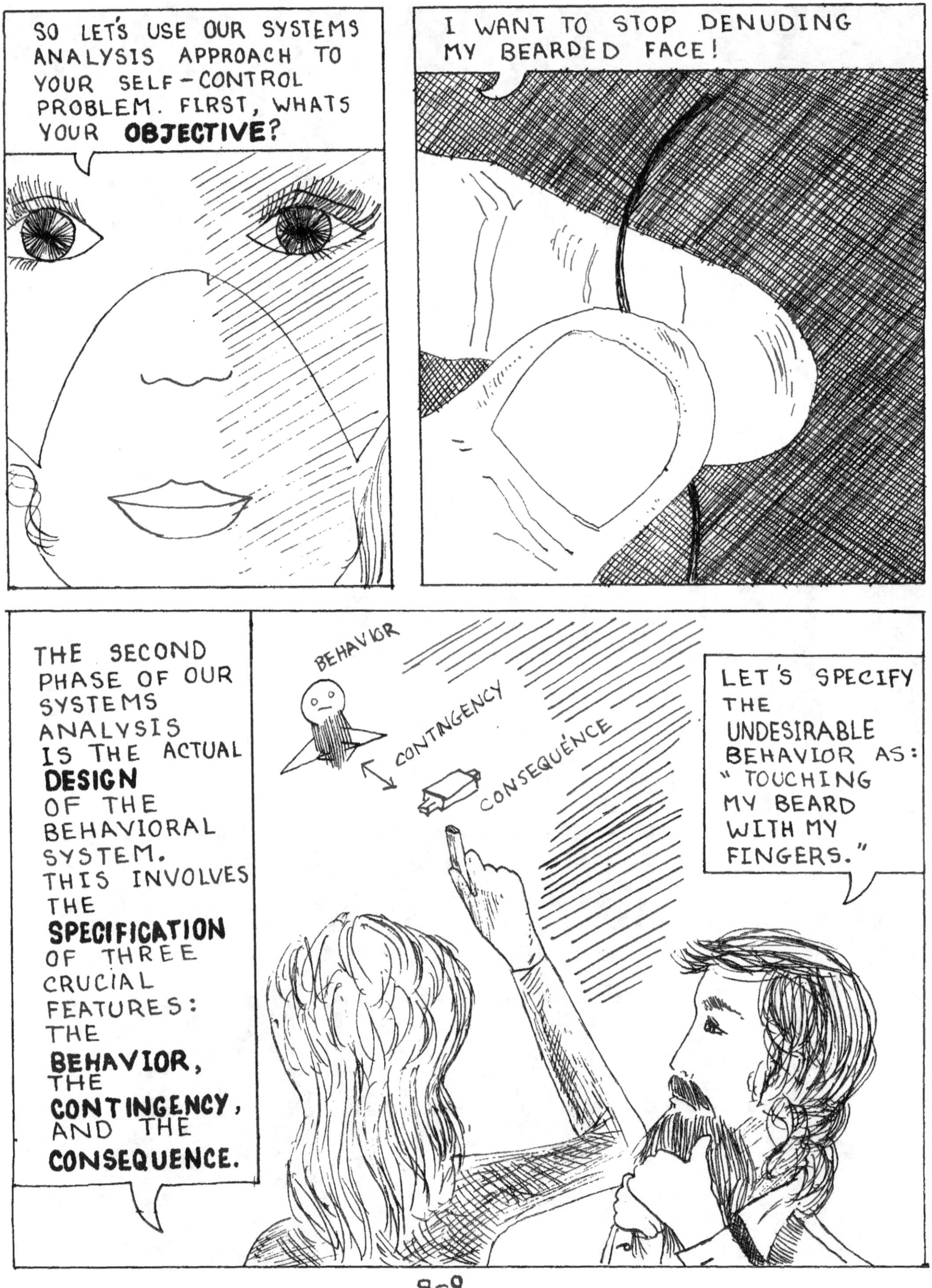

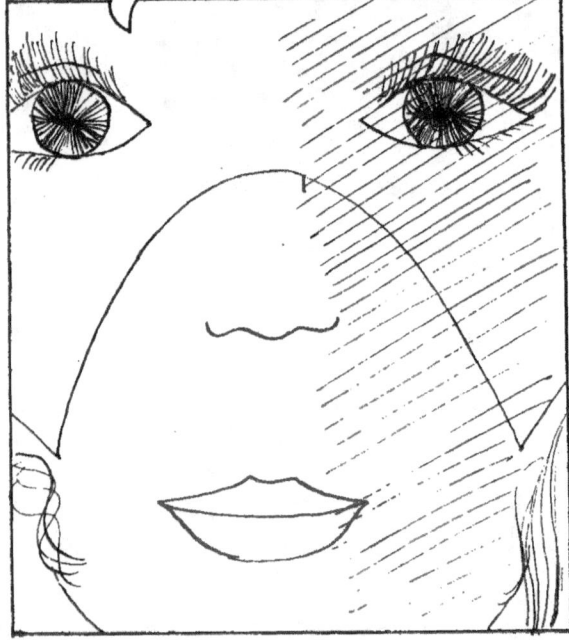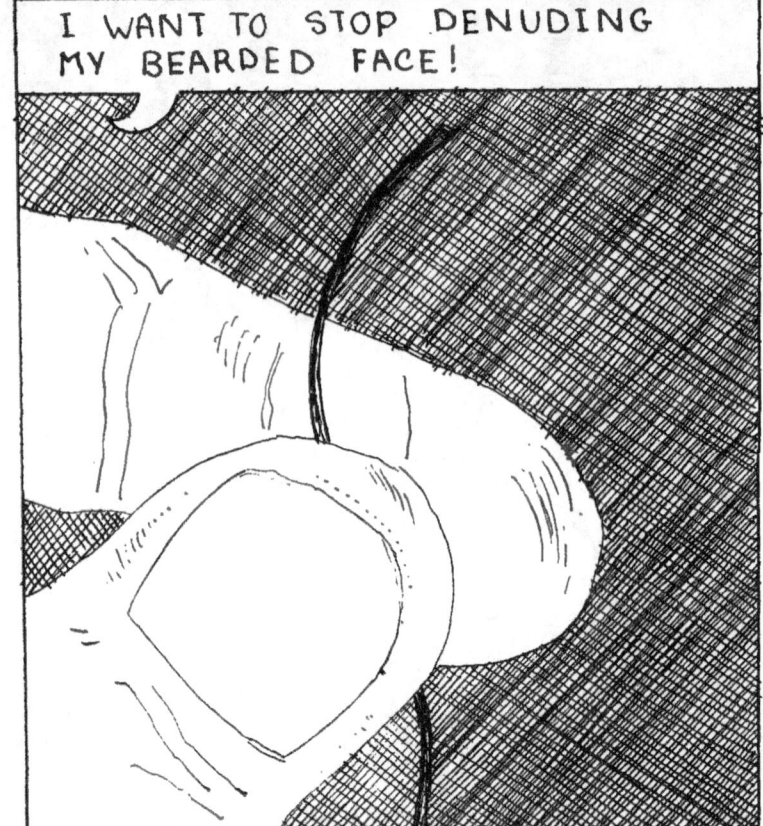

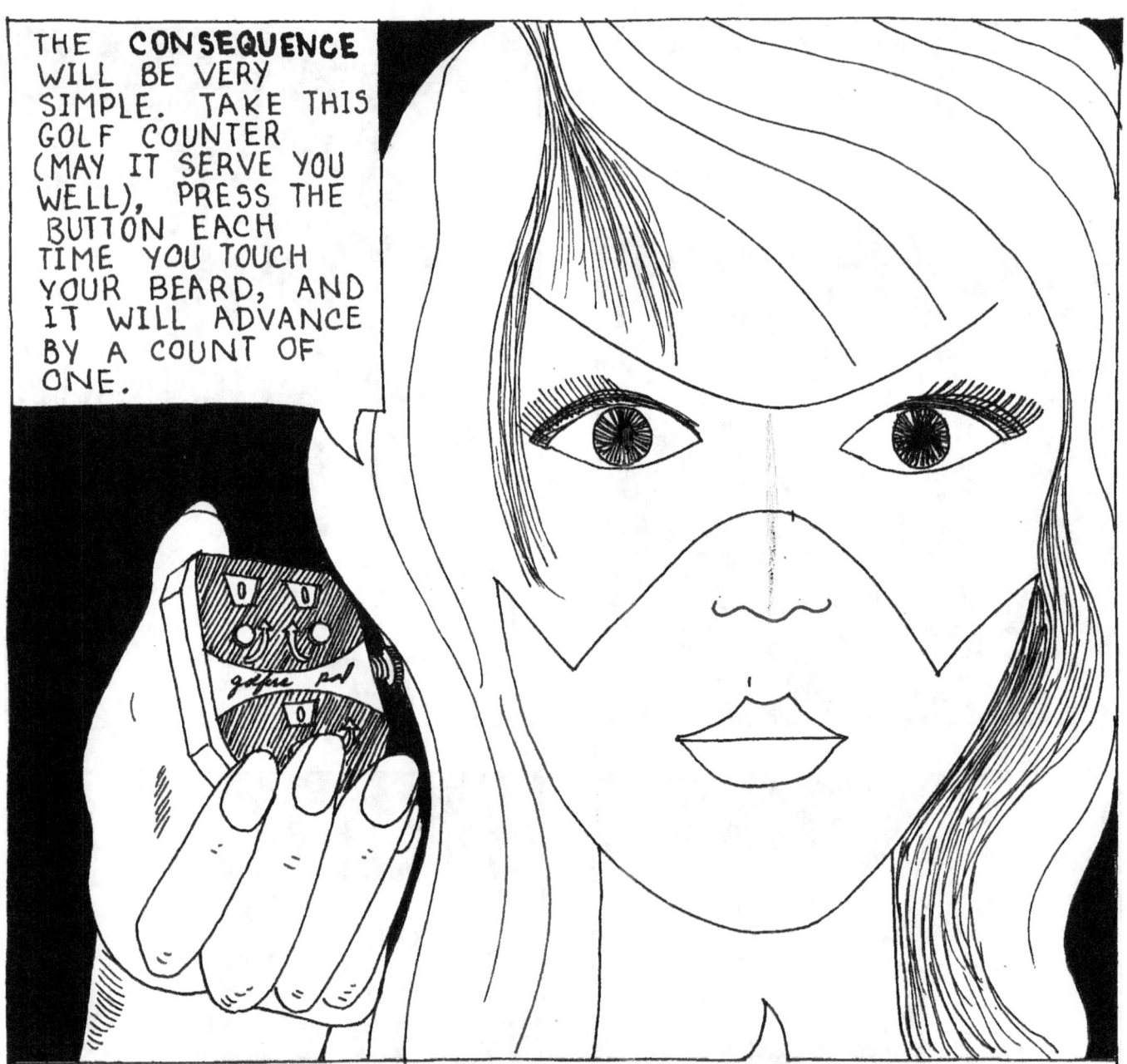

THE **CONSEQUENCE** WILL BE VERY SIMPLE. TAKE THIS GOLF COUNTER (MAY IT SERVE YOU WELL), PRESS THE BUTTON EACH TIME YOU TOUCH YOUR BEARD, AND IT WILL ADVANCE BY A COUNT OF ONE.

AT THE END OF THE DAY YOU LOOK AT THE COUNTER TO SEE HOW MANY TIMES YOU'VE EMITTED THE UNDESIRABLE BEHAVIOR OF TOUCHING YOUR BEARD. THEN PLOT THE TOTAL ON A GRAPH SO THAT FOR EACH DAY YOU'LL HAVE A RECORD OF THE NUMBER OF TIMES YOU TOUCHED YOUR BEARD. YOU MIGHT ALSO KEEP TRACK OF THE NUMBER OF TIMES YOU ACTUALLY PULLED THE HAIRS OUT OF YOUR BEARD.

NOW THAT WE'VE **SPECIFIED** THE THREE FEATURES OF THE **DESIGN**, NAMELY, THE _____, _____ AND _____, YOU NEED TO **IMPLEMENT** THE PROCEDURE. IN OTHER WORDS, GET ON WITH IT. RECORD THE DATA ON YOUR GRAPH SO WE CAN TEST THE PROCEDURE.

RECAP

1. Behavior is controlled by its consequences. Therefore, when the consequences are changed or eliminated, behavior changes. This was illustrated when the Beard Molester tried to discard the golf counter.

2. Self-control really means arranging events that will control your own behavior. Behavior is controlled by its consequences, not by will-power. What we commonly call will-power is behavior that is controlled by consequences rather than by some source of internal strength. We acquire "will-power" (behavior) by being punished for failure to "exhibit" it and by being reinforced when we "exhibit" it.

OBJECTIVES

1. Long-term consequences are usually not as powerful as frequent, small reinforcers.
   a) true
   b) false

2. To deal with self-control problems we should
   a) try harder.
   b) add some immediate consequences for our behavior.
   c) learn to forgive ourselves when we fail.
   d) find an outstanding spouse.

3. The design of a behavioral system involves the specification of _____.
   a) behavior
   b) consequence
   c) contingencies
   d) b & c
   e) all of the above

4. After the behavioral system is designed and implemented, it is necessary to _____.
   a) change the procedure
   b) test the procedure
   c) specify behavior, consequence, and contingency
   d) none of the above

5. Reinforcement can have two sources: intrinsic and extrinsic. A behavior is maintained by intrinsic reinforcement (either positive or negative) if the basic behavior itself is reinforcing to the individual. A behavior is maintained by extrinsic reinforcement (either positive or negative) if some additional consequence (other than the behavior) is necessary to maintain that behavior.

6. If you read Con. Man. because you are working for a grade, then reading Con. Man. is maintained by _____ reinforcement.
   a) intrinsic
   b) extrinsic
   c) both intrinsic and extrinsic

7. If you read Con. Man. because you enjoy the reading (either the stories or learning the principles of contingency management or both), then reading Con. Man. is maintained by _____ reinforcement.
   a) intrinsic
   b) extrinsic
   c) both intrinsic and extrinsic

8. If you read Con. Man for the grade, AND you like the stories (they are reinforcing to you), then reading is maintained by _____ reinforcement.
   a) intrinsic
   b) extrinsic
   c) both intrinsic and extrinsic

ANSWERS

1. a; 2. b; 3. e; 4. b; 6. b; 7. a; 8. c.

WHY? SO OUR GRADUATES CAN LEAD WORTHWHILE AND PRODUCTIVE LIVES, SO THEY CAN MAKE GREATER CONTRIBUTIONS BOTH TO SOCIETY AND TO THEMSELVES. BUT..... WHY ARE WE GOING THROUGH THIS PROLOGUE? IT SEEMS KIND OF SILLY. IT SEEMS LIKE WE'RE SAYING THE OBVIOUS, THE TRIVIAL, WITH WHICH EVERYONE CAN AGREE.

YES. EVERYONE AGREES UNTIL THEY THINK ABOUT THE IMPLICATIONS. THIS MEANS THAT WE'RE TRYING TO ELIMINATE ALL ARTIFICIAL BARRIERS TO HIGH STUDENT ACHIEVEMENT. WE'RE TRYING TO CHANGE THE PROCESS OF EDUCATION SO THAT IT IS NOT A SERIES OF OBSTACLES WHICH A STUDENT MUST OVERCOME. THIS WILL MEAN MUCH EXPERIMENTATION AND PLAIN HARD WORK TO DESIGN AND IMPLEMENT AN EDUCATIONAL SYSTEM. THIS SYSTEM MAY BE NEW, STRANGE, AND POSSIBLY UPSETTING TO MANY PEOPLE.

I'M VERY UPSET!

During the past few years, we have been using **SYSTEMS ANALYSIS** to develop an exciting and effective, but controversial new educational technology. We have been trying to make mass education excellent education. We have been trying to eliminate unhealthy competition between students and instead have all students compete with an absolute standard of excellence. We have had considerable success using this technology, **CONTINGENCY MANAGEMENT**, in individual courses.

At Western Michigan University, we finally got the courage to implement a **contingency management** system for an entire curriculum.

Our program is called:

STUDENT CENTERED EDUCATION PROJECT

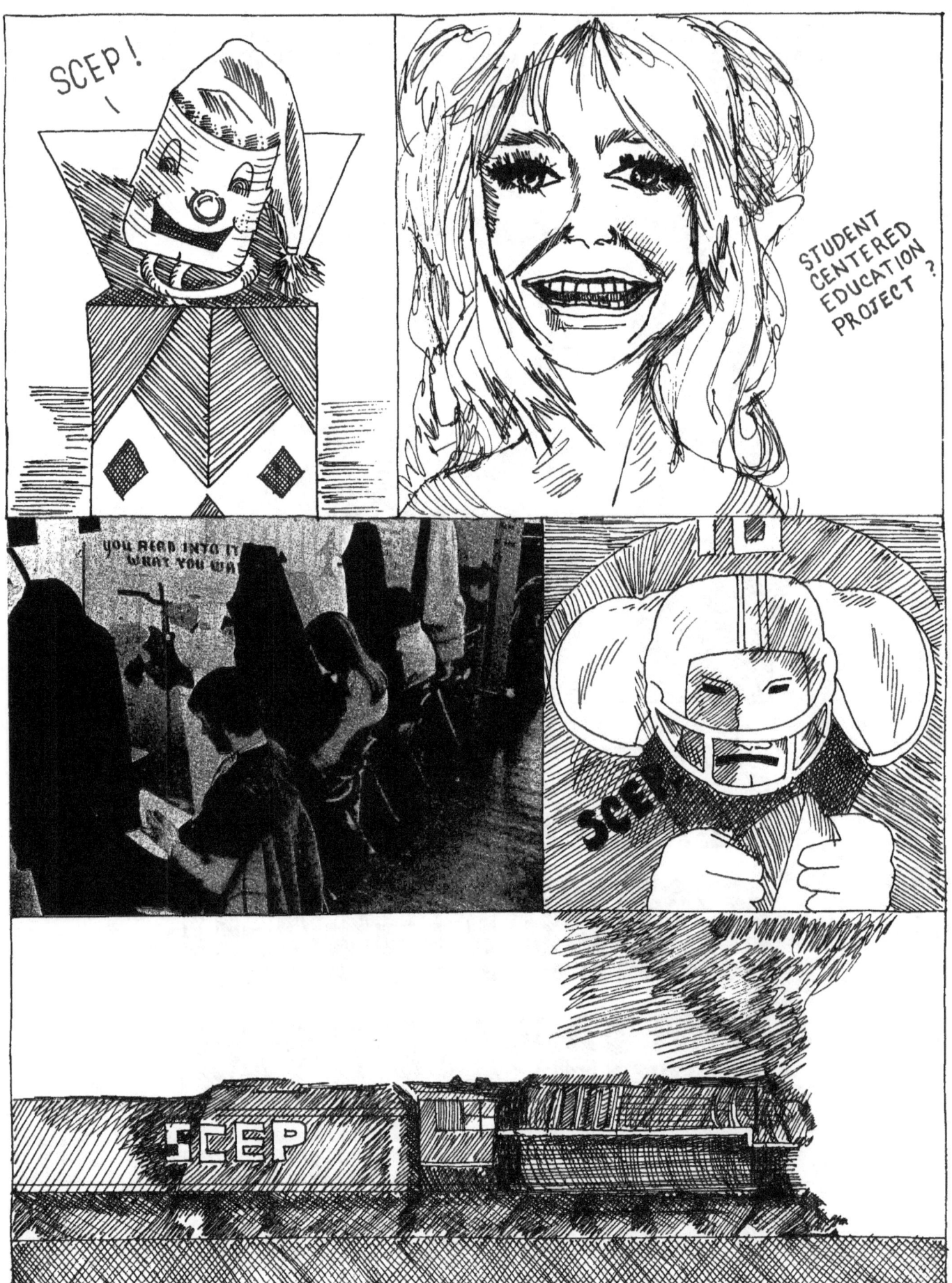

THIS EXPERIMENTAL PROJECT WAS IMPLEMENTED DURING THE FALL SEMESTER OF 1969. THE CORE OF THIS PROJECT IS 35 STUDENTS WHO VOLUNTEERED TO TAKE ALL OR MOST OF THEIR COURSES IN THE PROJECT. THEY HAD ALL HAD PREVIOUS EXPERIENCE WITH SINGLE COURSES TAUGHT USING CONTINGENCY MANAGEMENT. ON THE BASIS OF THIS EXPERIENCE, THEY WANTED TO BE IN A PROGRAM WHERE ALL OF THE COURSES WERE TAUGHT IN THAY MANNER.

THE STUDENT CENTERED EDUCATION PROJECT, OR SCEP, HAS TWO APARTMENT BUILDINGS WHICH ARE UNIVERSITY-APPROVED HOUSING AND SERVE AS DORMITORIES FOR 21 OF THE SCEP STUDENTS. EIGHT WOMEN LIVE IN THE WOMEN'S DORM, AND THIRTEEN MEN LIVE IN THE MEN'S DORM.

IT IS OUR FEELING AND THE FEELING OF THE STUDENTS THAT THE SCEP DORMS ARE AN IMPORTANT PART OF THE DESIGN. ALL OF THE STUDENTS LIVING IN THESE DORMS HAVE COMMON GOALS AND INTERESTS. THEY ARE ALL COMMITTED TO SPENDING A GREATER THAN AVERAGE AMOUNT OF TIME ON THEIR ACADEMIC WORK.

THE STUDENT CENTERED STUDY CENTER IS CONVENIENTLY LOCATED IN 201 CAMPUS SCHOOL, ONLY TWO BLOCKS AWAY FROM THE SCEP DORMS. THE SPACE BEING USED IS PART OF THE RESEARCH FACILITIES OF THE MANAGEMENT DEPARTMENT AT WESTERN MICHIGAN UNIVERSITY.

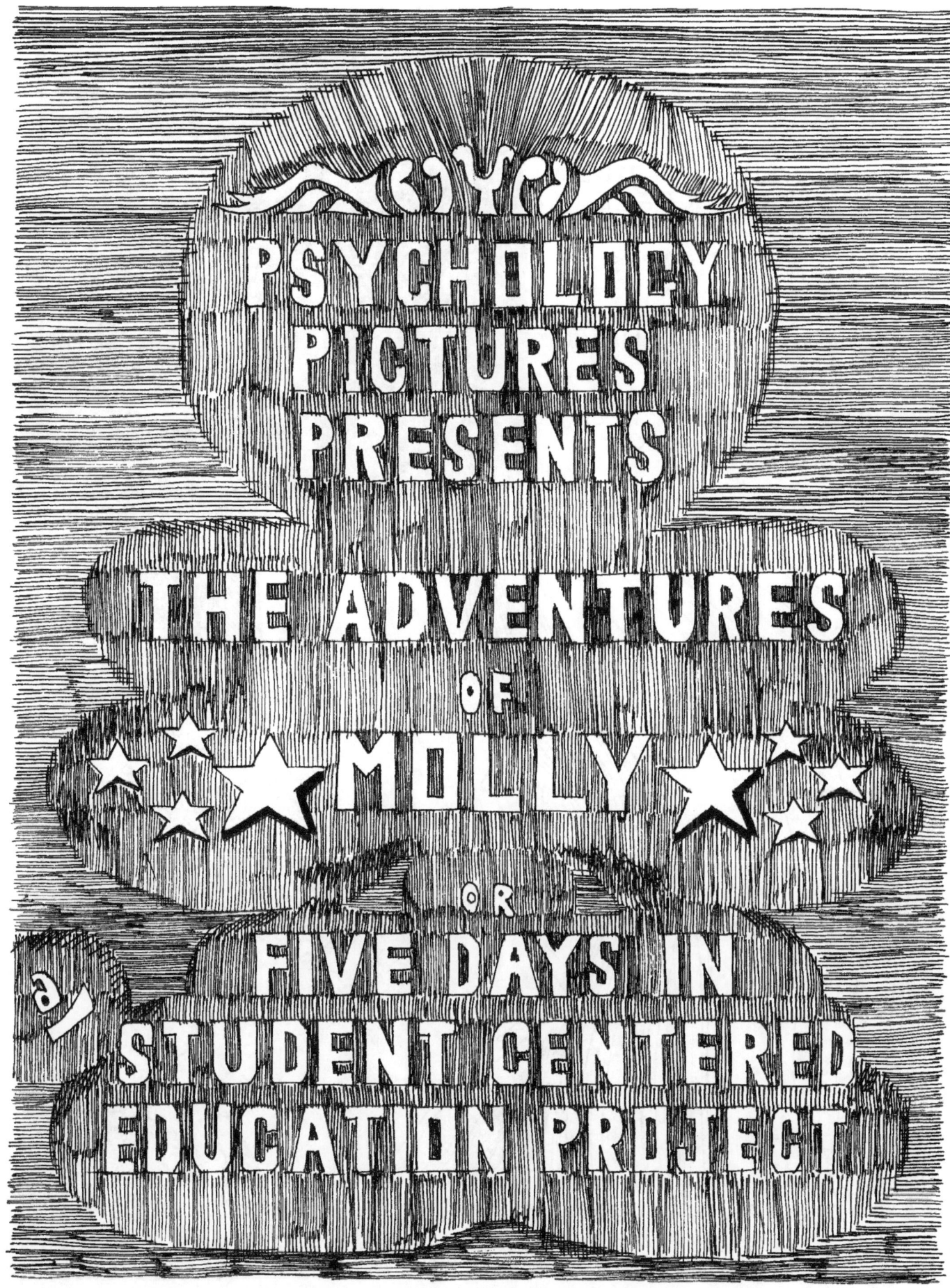

ONE OF THE FIRST THINGS MOLLY DOES ON ARRIVING AT THE STUDY CENTER IS TO CHECK ON THE MORNING COFFEE SUPPLY.

THEN SHE PICKS UP THE STUDY OBJECTIVES FOR THE READING ASSIGNMENT FOR THE FIRST COURSE OF THE DAY, DR. MALOTT'S PSYCHOLOGY 160.

THESE READING OBJECTIVES, OR STUDY GUIDES, ARE A CRUCIAL PART OF OUR EDUCATIONAL DESIGN. THEY SPECIFY, AS CLEARLY AS POSSIBLE WHAT BEHAVIOR THE STUDENT SHOULD ACQUIRE FROM EACH READING ASSIGNMENT.

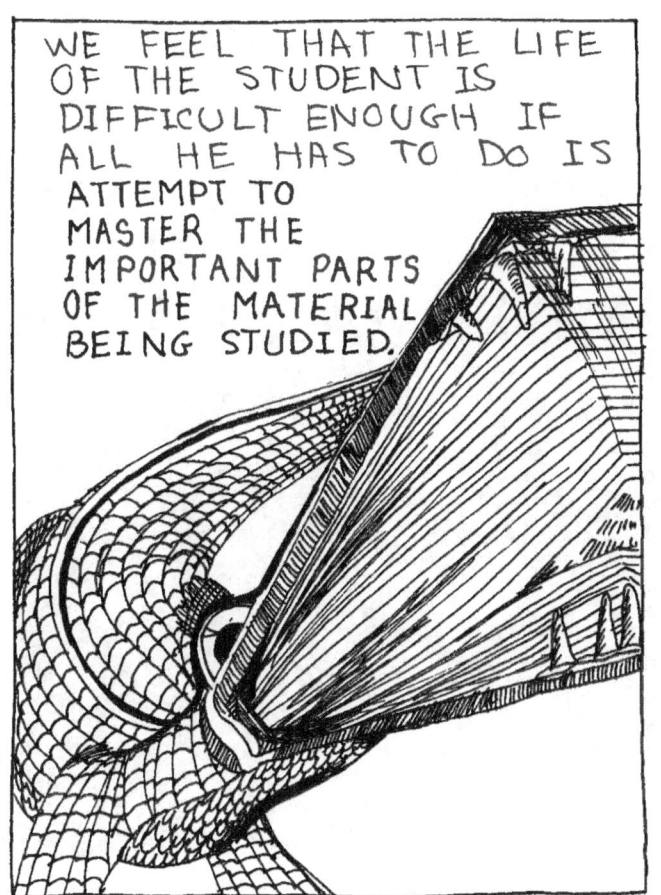

IT'S 8:15 AND TIME FOR THE FIRST CLASS TO START. MOLLY TAKES HER COFFEE AND READING OBJECTIVES TO HER STUDY CARREL.

INCIDENTALLY, THESE PORTABLE CARRELS WERE BUILT AND PAINTED BY THE STUDENTS.

SHE BRIEFLY GLANCES OVER THE OBJECTIVES AND THEN SETTLES DOWN TO ABOUT 30 MINUTES OF READING. AFTER READING THE ASSIGNMENT, SHE GOES OVER THE OBJECTIVES MORE THOROUGHLY TO INSURE THAT SHE CAN ANSWER ALL OF THE QUESTIONS. AT ONE POINT IT IS NECESSARY TO CALL ON JERRY SHOOK, THE TEACHING APPRENTICE, FOR HELP.

FINALLY, SHE WRITES DOWN THE ANSWERS TO THE READING OBJECTIVES AND STUDIES THEM.

ONE OF THE RESULTS OF THE PROJECT IS THAT WE HAVE BEEN ABLE TO EMPIRICALLY MEASURE, AT FIRST HAND, STUDENT STUDY BEHAVIOR UNDER OPTIMAL CONDITIONS. WE ARE NOW BEGINNING TO GET A GOOD IDEA ABOUT THE AMOUNT OF MATERIAL THAT STUDENTS CAN MASTER IN A STUDY PERIOD. FOR ALMOST ALL OUR COURSES, IT HAS BEEN MUCH LESS THAN WE HAD ANTICIPATED. IN THIS PSYCHOLOGY COURSE, WE HAVE FOUND THAT 7-10 PAGES OF A STANDARD TEXT ARE ALL THAT A STUDENT CAN REASONABLY ASSIMILATE IN A 40 MINUTE STUDY PERIOD.

AT 8:45 JERRY PASSES OUT THE QUIZ OVER THE DAY'S READING. WE ARE NOW IN THE PROCESS OF TRYING TO DESIGN MOST OF OUR OBJECTIVES AND QUIZZES SO THAT THEY WILL BE CONCEPTUAL IN NATURE AND CANNOT BE ANSWERED ON THE BASIS OF ROTE MEMORIZATION. THIS SORT OF CONCEPTUAL TEACHING IS A DIFFICULT TASK.

WHEN THE QUIZZES HAVE BEEN ANSWERED AND COLLECTED, STUDENTS RECEIVE IMMEDIATE FEEDBACK AS JERRY READS THE CORRECT ANSWERS. SHORTLY THEREAFTER, THE GRADES WILL BE POSTED, SO THAT THE STUDENTS ALWAYS KNOW WHERE THEY STAND.

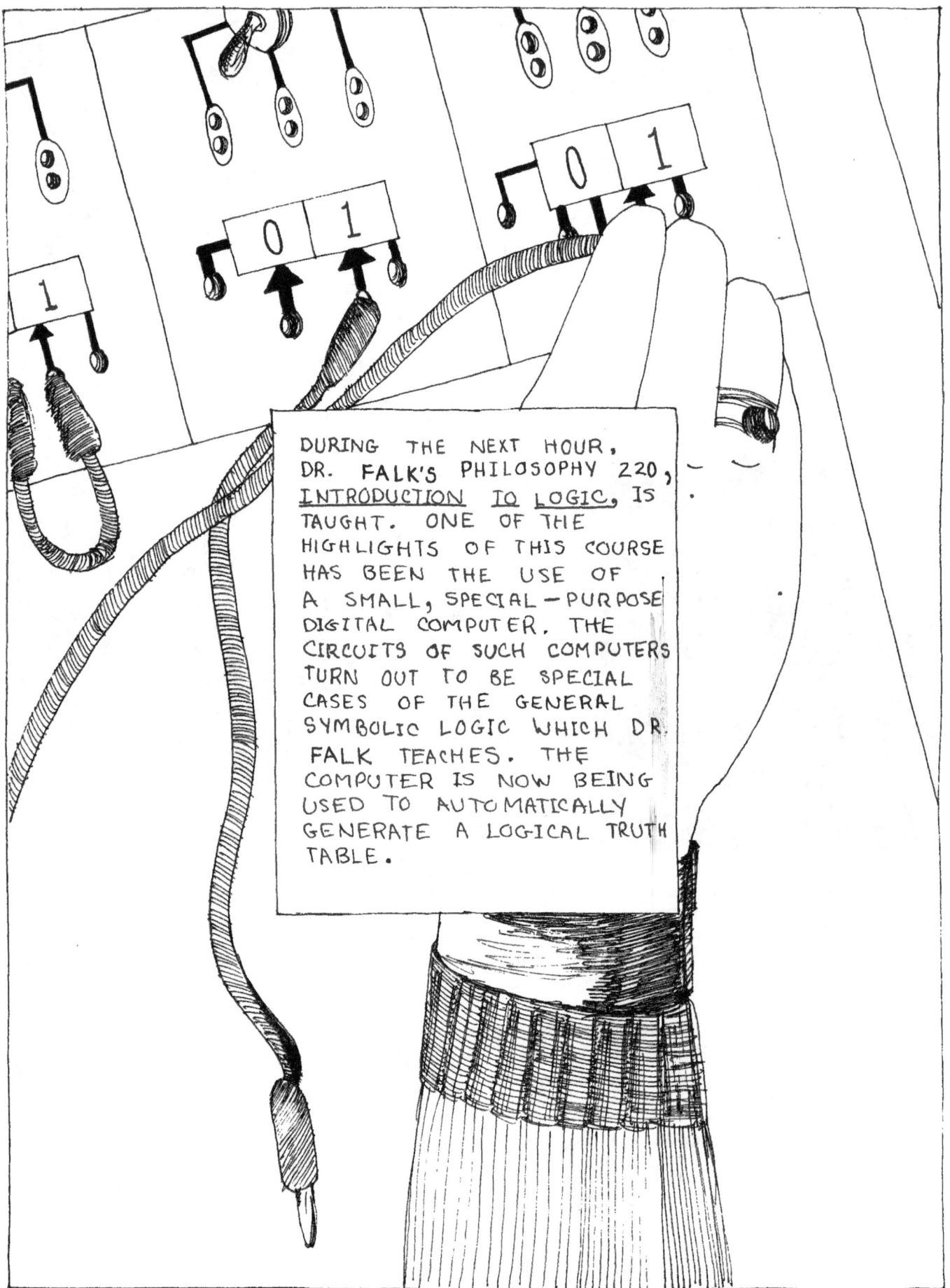

Possibly the most challenging course in the curriculum has been Dr. Keenan's Management 300: <u>Fundamentals of Management</u>. He is attempting to take the management course out of the business context and teach it from a much more general point of view. He is teaching general systems design and systems analysis. Because of the special interests of our students, the emphasis is on social or behavioral systems such as mental hospitals, classrooms, and families.

NOTICE THAT DURING THE FIRST FOUR HOURS OF THE DAY, THE STUDENT DOES NOT HAVE ANY DIRECT CONTACT WITH HIS PROFESSORS. HE DOES COME INTO INDIRECT CONTACT WITH THEM THROUGH THE TEXTS WHICH THEY SELECTED, THROUGH THE READING OBJECTIVES, AND THROUGH THE TEACHING APPRENTICES.

WE ARE FINALLY BEGINNING TO THROW OFF THE CONSTRAINTS OF OUR HISTORY.

WITH THE INVENTION OF THE PRINTING PRESS, IT IS NO LONGER NECESSARY TO RELY PRIMARILY ON THE ORAL TRADITION (I.E. LECTURES) FOR THE TRANSMISSION OF OUR CULTURE. THIS NEWFANGLED DEVICE CALLED THE TEXT BOOK IS REALLY WONDERFUL FOR THAT PURPOSE.

WE HAVE DISCOVERED THE BOOK — A SIGNIFICANT ADVANCE IN EDUCATIONAL TECHNOLOGY.

BUT WE ARE NOT COMPLETELY EMANCIPATED.

..... AND THE FACULTY WERE AFRAID THE STUDENTS, EATING THEIR LUNCHES, WOULD BE DISTRACTED FROM THE LECTURES.

THE LUNCHEON LECTURES VARY CONSIDERABLY IN FORMAT:
   DR. HINKEL FREQUENTLY PLAYS AUDIO TAPES BY ROCK MUSICIANS, SUCH AS BOB DYLAN, AND THEN ANALYZES THE LYRICS AS EXAMPLES OF MODERN POETRY.
   DR. MALOTT CONDUCTS INFORMAL DISCUSSIONS OR HAS GUEST LECTURERS. DR. FALK DISCUSSES DIFFICULTIES THE STUDENTS HAVE HAD WITH THE WEEKS ASSIGNMENT, AND DR. KEENAN PRESENTS ADDITIONAL EXAMPLES OF SYSTEMS ANALYSES.

AH GET BORN SHORT PANTS GET DRESSED GET

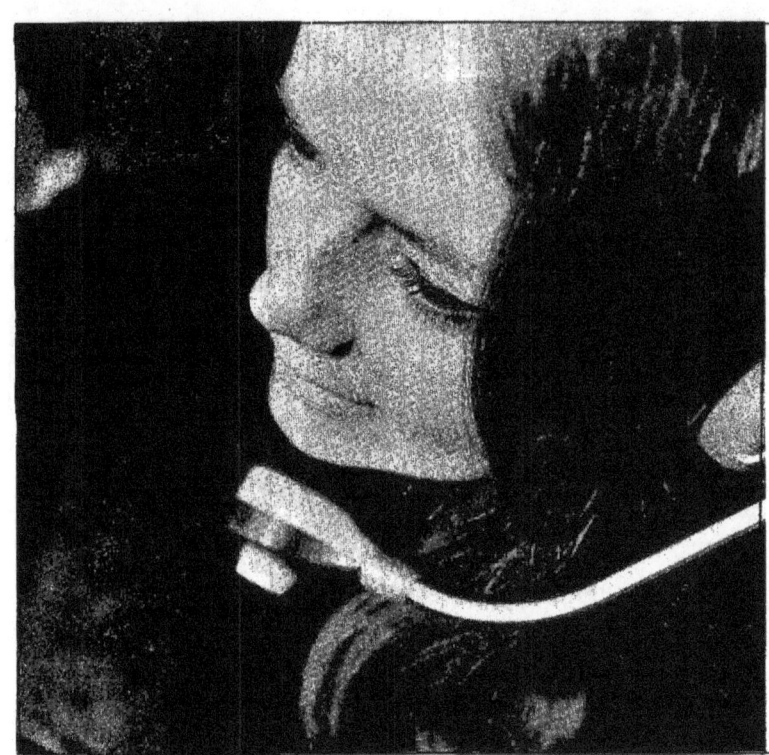

AT 1:15 THE STUDENTS HAVE A TWO HOUR PSYCHOLOGY PRACTICUM. THEY MAY STUDY AS APPRENTICE THERAPISTS UNDER DR. HITZING AT THE KALAMAZOO STATE HOSPITAL OR AS APPRENTICE TEACHERS IN INTRODUCTORY PSYCHOLOGY UNDER DR. MALOTT.

THE STUDENTS FEEL THAT THESE APPRENTICESHIPS ARE THE MOST VALUABLE PART OF THEIR EDUCATION. THEY DO NOT HAVE TO WAIT UNTIL THEY GRADUATE FROM COLLEGE TO MAKE WORTHWHILE CONTRIBUITIONS TO MANKIND.

AFTER TWO HOURS AT THE STATE HOSPITAL, MOLLY RETURNS TO DO A ONE-HOUR WRITING ASSIGNMENT. A ONE-PAGE, TYPEWRITTEN ESSAY IS REQUIRED PER WEEK FOR EACH COURSE. IN THIS ESSAY, THE STUDENT IS EXPECTED TO PRESENT AN ORIGINAL IDEA, ANALYSIS, CRITICISM, OR INTERPRETATION. RELEVANT TO THE WEEK'S ASSIGNMENTS. IN SHORT, THE STUDENT IS EXPECTED TO BE CREATIVE. SUGGESTIONS ARE GIVEN AS TO THE KIND OF TOPIC WHICH MIGHT BE APPROPRIATE FOR THE WEEK'S ESSAY, BUT THE STUDENT IS USUALLY FREE TO SELECT HIS OWN TOPIC.

IF A STUDENT HAS FAILED TO OBTAIN A SATISFACTORY GRADE ON ONE OR MORE OF THE DAILY QUIZZES, HE HAS THE OPPORTUNITY TO ATTEND MAKE-UP SESSIONS STARTING AT 7:00 P.M. THAT EVENING BACK AT THE STUDY CENTER. HERE HE STUDIES THE MATERIAL AGAIN FOR 40 MINUTES AND THEN TAKES A NEW QUIZ. THESE REMEDIAL SESSIONS ARE AVAILABLE FROM 7 UNTIL 10 EVERY NIGHT. IN ADDITION, HE HAS THE OPPORTUNITY TO REWRITE EACH OF HIS WRITING ASSIGNMENTS UNTIL IT IS ACCEPTABLE. OUR PHILOSOPHY IS TO TRY TO ARRANGE OUR EDUCATIONAL PROCEDURES SO THAT ALL STUDENTS HAVE AN OPPORTUNITY TO ACHIEVE EXCELLENCE, EVEN THOUGH IT MAY TAKE SOME A LITTLE LONGER THAN OTHERS.

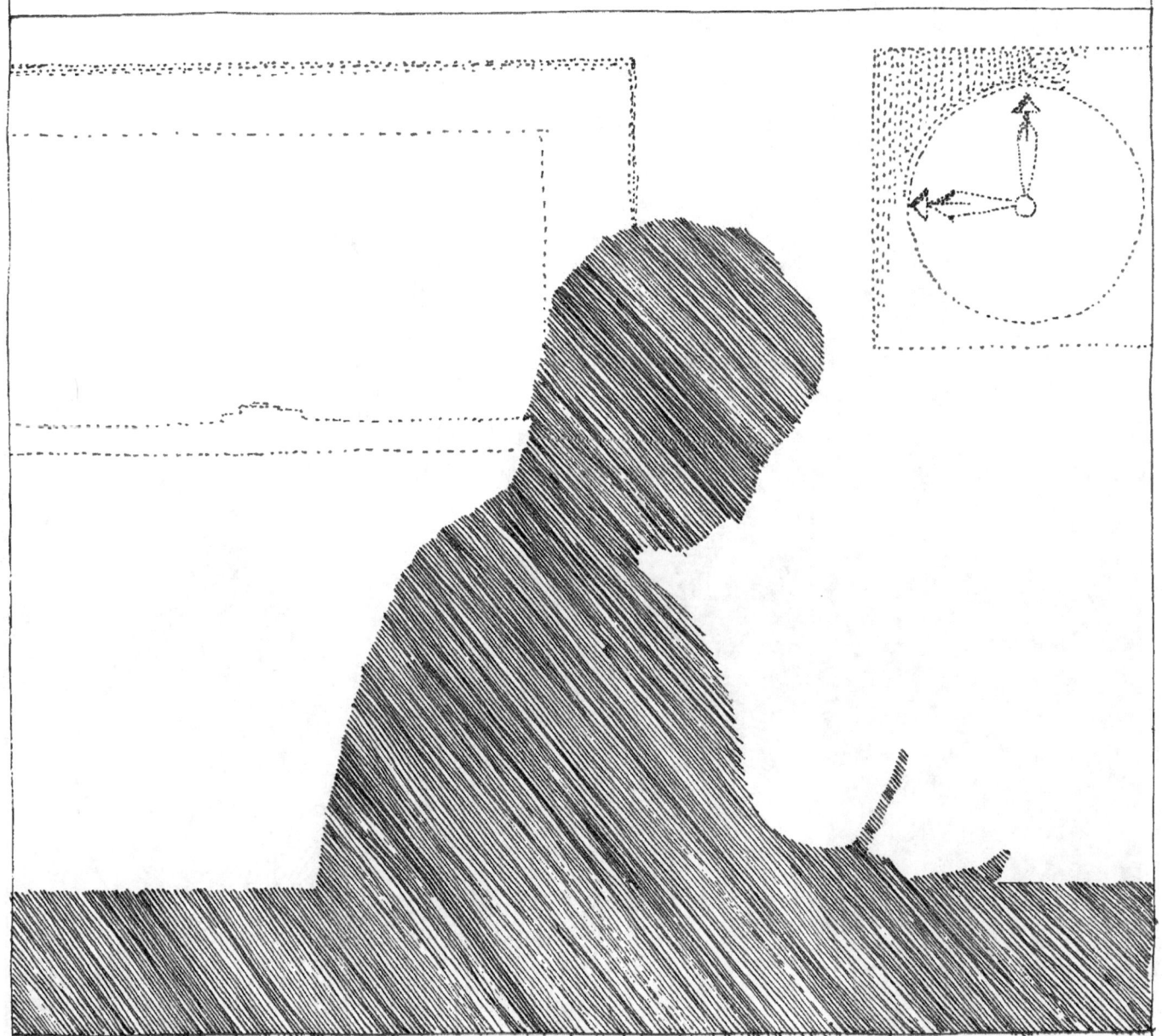

FINALLY, THE STUDENTS WORK AN AVERAGE OF ONE-AND-A-HALF HOURS PER DAY ON THEIR ARTS AND IDEAS PROJECTS. MOST OF THEM INVOLVE MAKING SLIDE TAPE SHOWS. THIS CONSTITUTES AN IDEAL PROJECT, AS IT REQUIRES INTEGRATION OF THE WRITTEN, SPOKEN, MUSICAL, AND VISUAL ARTS. IN ADDITION, THE STUDENTS ARE LEARNING AN IMPORTANT MULTI-MEDIA TECHNIQUE.

"WATCH THE BIRDIE!"

TO SUMMARIZE WHAT WE HAVE COVERED SO FAR: WE ARE TRYING TO DESIGN AN OPTIMUM LEARNING SYSTEM.

FIRST, THE STUDENTS LIVE WITH OTHER STUDENTS WHO SHARE THEIR SAME STRONG ACADEMIC COMMITMENT.

SECOND, WE REALIZE THAT EVEN AN OPTIMUM DORMITORY ENVIRONMENT IS APPROPRIATE FOR SLEEPING, EATING, AND RECREATION, BUT NOT FOR STUDYING. THEREFORE, WE HAVE ATTEMPTED TO PROVIDE A SEPARATE ENVIRONMENT WHICH IS BETTER SUITED FOR THEIR STUDYING — NAMELY, THE STUDENT CENTERED STUDY CENTER.

THIRD, WE HAVE MADE THE ASSIGNMENT OF SUCH A SIZE THAT THE STUDENTS CAN REASONABLY BE EXPECTED TO MASTER THEM.

FOURTH, WE PROVIDE CLEAR STUDY OBJECTIVES FOR EACH ASSIGNMENT, SO THAT HE CAN, IN FACT, UNDERSTAND WHAT HE IS EXPECTED TO MASTER.

FIFTH, ONE OF THE MOST IMPORTANT FEATURES IS THAT THE ASSIGNMENTS ARE DAILY AND THAT THERE IS A DAILY QUIZ TO ENCOURAGE DAILY STUDY OF ASSIGNMENTS. THE USUAL PROCEDURE OF TWO OR THREE HOUR EXAMS SPREAD THROUGHOUT THE SEMESTER FOSTERS POOR STUDY BEHAVIOR, SUCH AS STUDYING ONLY THE NIGHT BEFORE THE EXAM. THE RESULT IS THAT MUCH OF THE MATERIAL IS NOT EVEN READ, AND THAT WHICH IS READ IS POORLY UNDERSTOOD.

SIXTH, IMMEDIATELY AFTER THE QUIZ THE STUDENTS ARE GIVEN KNOWLEDGE OF RESULTS IN THE FORM OF THE CORRECT ANSWERS READ BY THE TEACHING APPRENTICE. A SHORT TIME LATER, SCORES ARE POSTED ON THE BULLETIN BOARD.
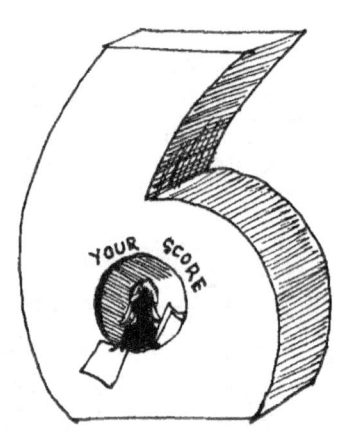

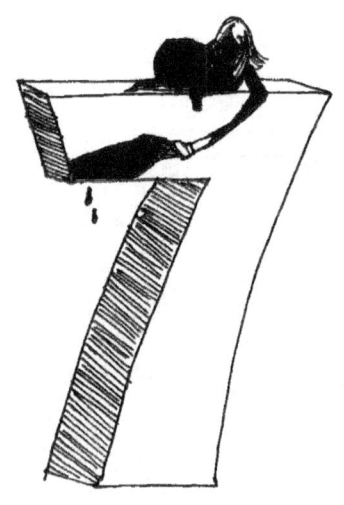
SEVENTH, AND FINALLY, THE STUDENTS HAVE BEEN ENCOURAGED TO DECORATE THEIR ENVIRONMENT SO THAT IT IS PLEASANT AND ATTRACTIVE TO THEM.

TO SUMMARIZE THE STUDENT'S TYPICAL DAILY ACTIVITY: HE SPENDS 4 HOURS IN READING, 1 IN LECTURE, 2 IN AN APPRENTICESHIP, 1 IN WRITING, AND 1½ ON AN ARTS AND IDEAS PROJECT. THIS IS A TOTAL OF 9½ HOURS PER DAY FOR FIVE DAYS A WEEK, OR 47½ HOURS PER WEEK. THE AMOUNT OF ADDITIONAL REMEDIAL WORK IN THE EVENING VARIES CONSIDERABLY AMONG STUDENTS.

Grades are used both as incentives and as indicators of accomplishment. We are constantly experimenting with different incentive systems. For example, this semester the system is quite complex. In order to receive the grade of "A" for the course, the student must earn 90% of his daily points for the reading quizzes, lecture attendance, writing assignments, and projects. A final exam will be given one week before the end of the term. If the student answers approximately 97% of his daily quiz questions correctly, then the final exam has no effect on his final course grade. Otherwise, it is weighed heavily. In addition, however, all students who get an "A" on the final exam are exempt from the last week of classes for the course. Those who get less than an "A" have demonstrated the need for additional remedial work during the final week. Next semester we will be testing a new system, but that's another story.

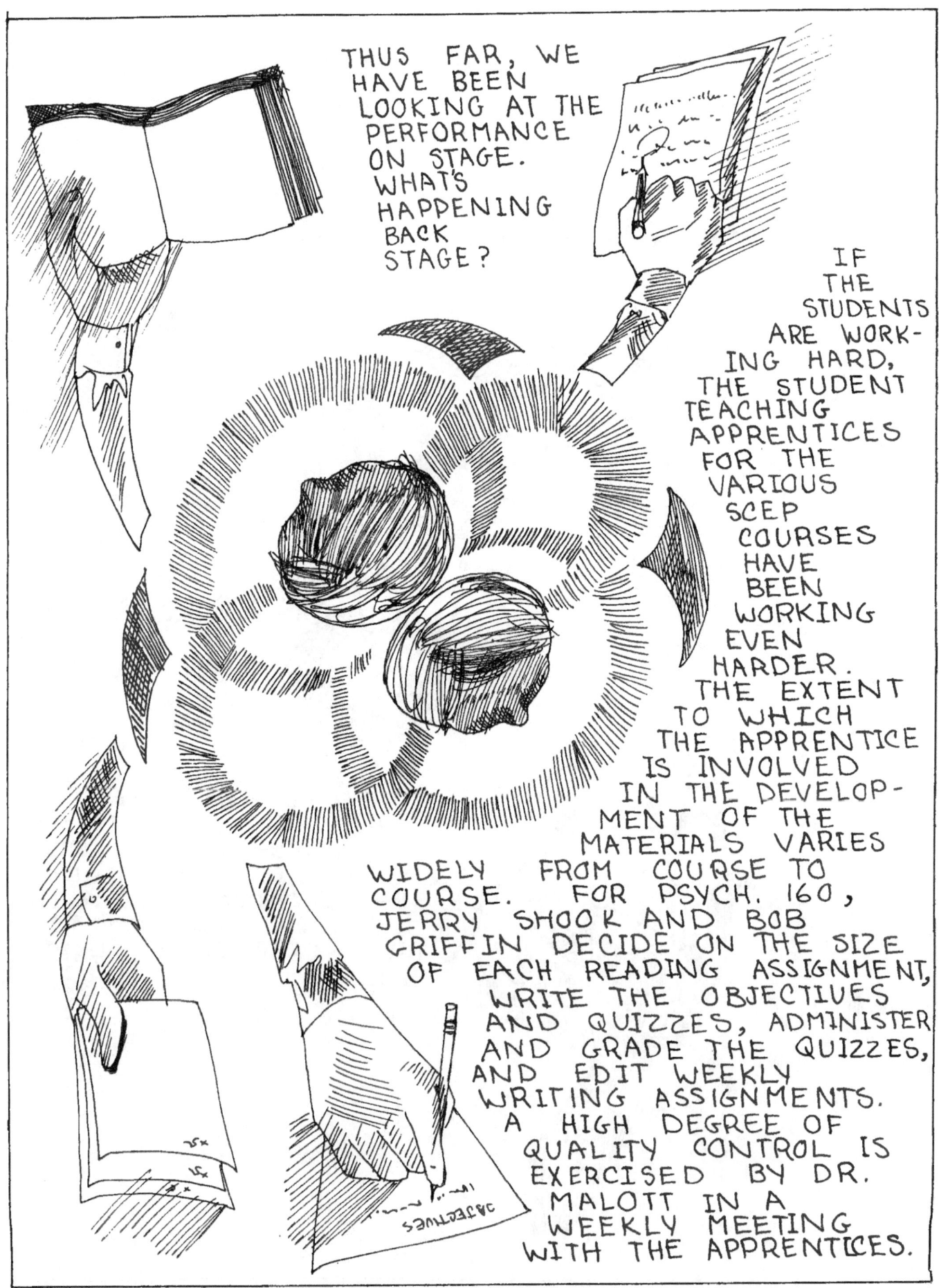

THUS FAR, WE HAVE BEEN LOOKING AT THE PERFORMANCE ON STAGE. WHAT'S HAPPENING BACK STAGE?

IF THE STUDENTS ARE WORKING HARD, THE STUDENT TEACHING APPRENTICES FOR THE VARIOUS SCEP COURSES HAVE BEEN WORKING EVEN HARDER. THE EXTENT TO WHICH THE APPRENTICE IS INVOLVED IN THE DEVELOPMENT OF THE MATERIALS VARIES WIDELY FROM COURSE TO COURSE. FOR PSYCH. 160, JERRY SHOOK AND BOB GRIFFIN DECIDE ON THE SIZE OF EACH READING ASSIGNMENT, WRITE THE OBJECTIVES AND QUIZZES, ADMINISTER AND GRADE THE QUIZZES, AND EDIT WEEKLY WRITING ASSIGNMENTS. A HIGH DEGREE OF QUALITY CONTROL IS EXERCISED BY DR. MALOTT IN A WEEKLY MEETING WITH THE APPRENTICES.

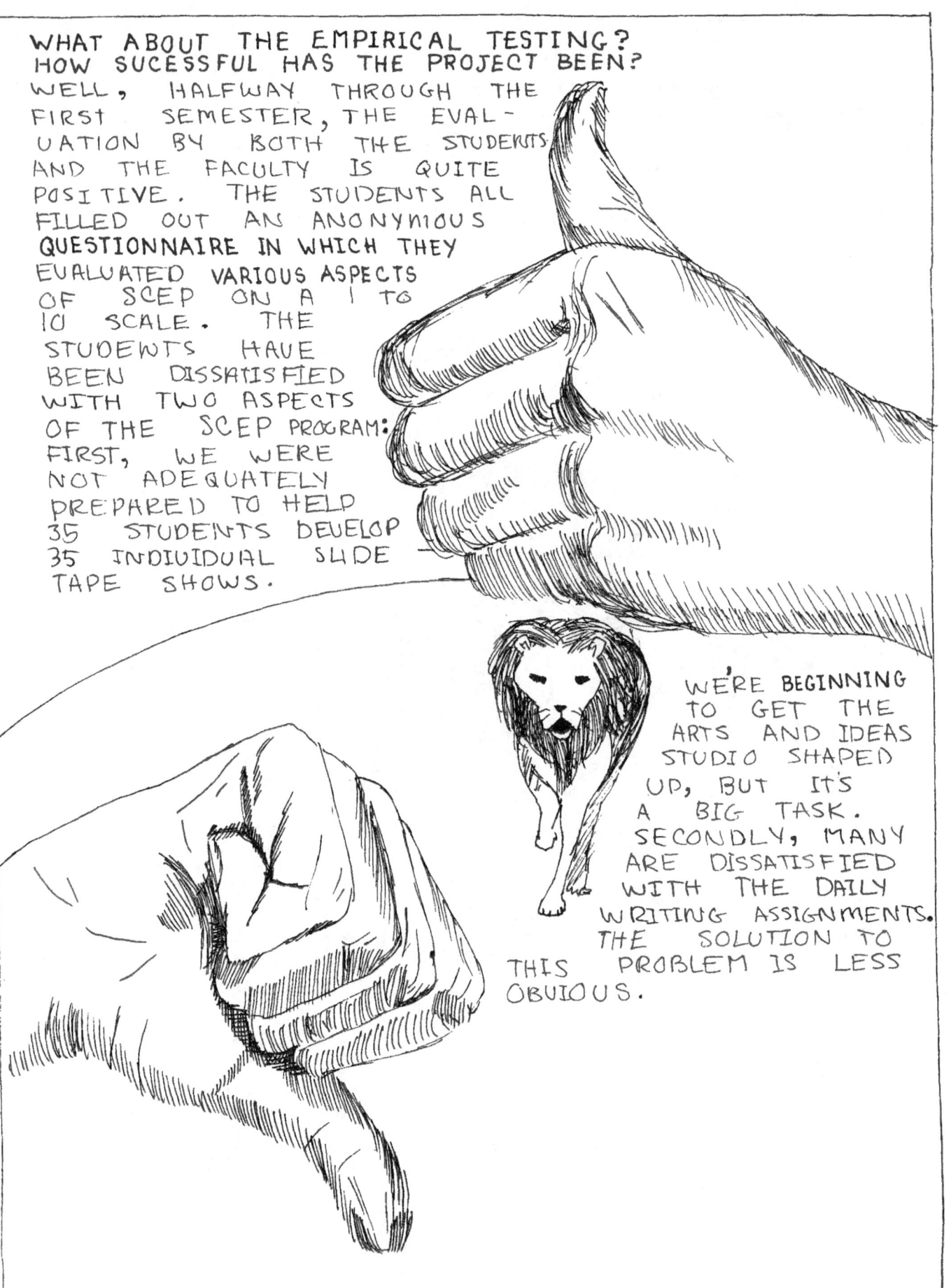

In comparison to traditional courses, the students rated the contents of the SCEP courses as vastly superior. They strongly prefer studying in the SCEP system, they learn much more in SCEP, they work much harder in SCEP, and they strongly prefer daily quizzes to hour exams. Although they are under slightly more pressure than students in traditional courses, most feel that the pressure is not too intense. There is considerable academic interaction among the SCEP students in the SCEP dorms, where they make much use of the technical vocabulary they are learning in SCEP.

A much more objective measure of satisfaction may be found in the fact that nearly all of the students are continuing in SCEP next term.

In general, however, many of the students will be taking fewer courses in SCEP next term than presently. The reason given is that some of the courses they need are not being offered in SCEP. None of the students has indicated a dissatisfaction with the SCEP teaching system. More data will be needed to confirm this.

All of the present faculty have verbally indicated satisfaction and are continuing with new courses next semester. In fact, two of the four faculty will be doubling their teaching load in SCEP.

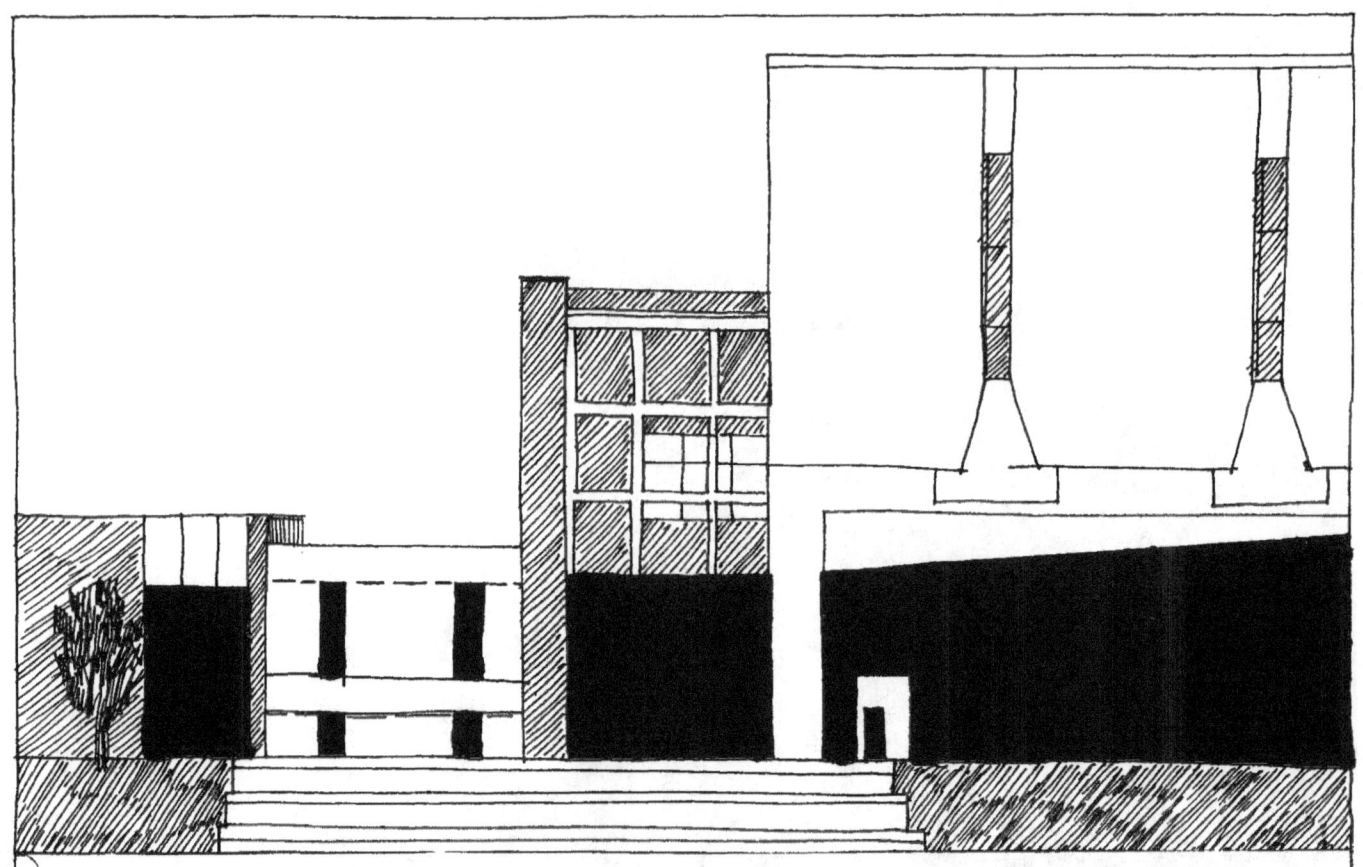

EDITOR'S NOTE

THIS PROGRESS REPORT WAS BASED ON THE FIRST SEMESTER OF THE PROJECT. AT THE TIME OF THIS WRITING, MAY 15, 1971, WE HAVE FINISHED THE FOURTH SEMESTER, AND HAVE GONE THROUGH FOUR CYCLES OF OUR SYSTEMS ANALYSIS PROCEDURE. MANY CHANGES HAVE BEEN MADE IN THE DETAILS, BUT THE BASIC APPROACH IS MUCH THE SAME.

OF THE FACULTY INITIALLY INVOLVED IN THE PROJECT, ROBERT HINKEL IS NO LONGER PARTICIPATING. THE FACULTY MOST RECENTLY INVOLVED IN THIS PROJECT ARE: ARTHUR FALK, ROBERT HARMON, WADE HITZING, ANTHONY GIOIA, RICHARD MALOTT, JACK MICHAEL, RICHARD POLASKI, GREGORY SHERIDAN, AND BRYCE ZENDUER.

WE ARE VERY GRATEFUL TO BE AT AN INSTITUTION WHICH ALLOWS AND ENCOURAGES EDUCATIONAL INNOVATION SUCH AS THIS.

RECAP

1. The preceding was an example of how an educational system can be designed by using the principles of contingency management and systems analysis.

2. The basic rules of contingency management were followed in SCEP.
    a. be consistent — the same grading and remedial contingencies were always in effect.
    b. think small — students were given relatively small reading assignments (7-10 pages for 40 minutes).
    c. establish functional behavior — students learned skills that would generalize to other academic areas, thus insuring a source of reinforcement for this type of behavior once the students left SCEP.
    d. reinforce each unit of the stimulus-response chain — after each reading unit and quiz (given daily), the students receive quiz scores.

3. The phases of Systems Analysis were used in the design and development of SCEP.
    a. state the primary objectives — teach as much as possible to as many as possible.

   b. specify behavior, contingency, and consequence (the three phases of contingency management) —
      1. Specification (in SCEP)
         a. behavior: high quiz performance
         b. contingencies: positive reinforcement, negative reinforcement, avoidance, punishment
         c. consequences: grades, remediation
      2. Observation (in SCEP)
         a. daily quizzes
         b. TA-student interaction
      3. Consequation (in SCEP)
         a. receiving grades
         b. remedial quiz attendance
   c. implement the procedure — SCEP is in progress.
   d. test the procedure — student achievement has been measured and evaluated
   e. change the procedure if necessary — SCEP has come a long way since this chapter was written. SCEP is on its way to its fifth semester, and many procedures and techniques are constantly evaluated and changed when necessary.

9 — 40

OBJECTIVES

1. According to CON. MAN., the goal of those in the teaching profession should be to:
   a) present material in a straightforward, logical manner.
   b) teach as much as possible to as many students as possible.
   c) weed out students who should spend their lives at manual labor.
   d) teach very little material to a few people, but do it well.

2. The purpose of reading objectives is to:
   a) indicate as clearly as possible the important points in each reading assignment.
   b) help students through texts which would otherwise not be understandable to them.
   c) remove the students' burden of deciding what is important and what is not important.
   d) a & c.
   e) all of the above.

3. The educational philosophy presented in this chapter is:
   a) some students don't belong in school and can better serve their country at manual labor.
   b) arrange educational procedures so that MOST students master the material.
   c) arrange educational procedures so that ALL students may achieve educational excellence.
   d) none of the above

4. It is desirable that students live with other students who share the same academic goals and interests.
   a) True
   b) False

5. Optimum dormitory environments always include a study center.
   a) True
   b) False

6. Assignments should be of a size that allows students to master the material in the time given.
   a) True
   b) False

7. It is not wise to provide reading objectives with each assignment.
   a) True
   b) False

8. Daily study of assignments is encouraged through the use of _____.
   a) daily assignments
   b) reading objectives for each assignment
   c) short reading assignments
   d) 2 to 3 hour exams
   e) daily quizzes

9. Immediate feedback for quiz behavior is provided by _____.
   a) knowledge of the correct answers
   b) posting of scores
   c) seminar discussions
   d) listening to tape recorders
   e) a & b

10. The immediate environment affects our behavior to a great extent. For this reason students should study in a(n) _____ environment.
    a) uncomfortable
    b) pleasant and attractive

11. In SCEP, grades are used as both _____ and _____.
    a) indicators of accomplishment; indicators of the world
    b) feedback; intrinsic reinforcers
    c) extrinsic reinforcers; intrinsic reinforcers
    d) incentives; indicators of accomplishment

12. In SCEP, grades indicate _____.
    a) intelligence
    b) employment potential
    c) I.Q.
    d) accomplishment

13. In SCEP, grades are used as incentives for academic behavior.
    a) True
    b) False

14. When grades are used as incentives, they are a form of _____ consequation.
    a) intrinsic
    b) extrinsic

15. What are the steps of Systems Analysis? (Circle all correct).
    a) state your primary objectives
    b) specify the behavior, contingency, and the consequences
    c) implement the procedure
    d) test the procedure
    e) change the procedure if indicated in the test

16. The three basic phases in contingency management are _____ , _____ , and _____ .
    (Circle all correct.)
    a) behavior
    b) observation
    c) consequation
    d) behavior application
    e) S. O. O.
    f) moderation
    g) consistency
    h) specification

17. In SCEP, the PRIMARY OBJECTIVE is to _____ .
    a) present material in a logical, straightforward manner
    b) decide which students aren't meant for college
    c) teach as much as possible to as many as possible
    d) teach little, but do it thoroughly

18. In SCEP, the BEHAVIOR SPECIFIED is _____ .
    a) listed (specified) in the objectives over the text material
    b) high quiz performances
    c) remedial quizzes
    d) immediate feedback
    e) a & b

19. In SCEP, the CONTINGENCIES are _____ . (Choose all that are correct.)
    a) negative reinforcement
    b) positive reinforcement
    c) avoidance
    d) escape
    e) punishment

20. The design of SCEP was based on Systems Analysis because the procedure was _____ .
    a) implemented
    b) tested
    c) changed after testing indicated a change
    d) a & b
    e) all of the above

ANSWERS

1. b; 2. e; 3. c; 4. a; 5. b; 6. a; 7. b; 8. e; 9. e; 10. b; 11. d; 12. d; 13. a; 14. b; 15. a, b, c, d, e; 16. b, c, h; 17. c; 18. e; 19. a, b, c, d, e; 20. e.

PSYCOLOGICAL CONFESSIONS

L. PULP PUBLISHING CO.

IN THIS ISSUE —

Confessions of a Scientist!

REMEMBER, SOME REWARDS OR REINFORCERS ARE *NATURAL* REINFORCERS— YOU MIGHT SAY WE WERE BORN THAT WAY. YOU MIGHT SAY THEY WERE WIRED IN AT THE FACTORY. THESE UNLEARNED REINFORCERS ARE CALLED *UNCONDITIONED REINFORCERS*, OR *PRIMARY REINFORCERS*.

OTHER REINFORCERS WERE ADDED AFTER WE LEFT THE FACTORY— THEY'RE THOSE LITTLE OPTIONS THAT ADD ZEST TO LIFE. THEY'RE ACQUIRED OR LEARNED, AND THEY'RE CALLED *CONDITIONED REINFORCERS* OR *LEARNED REINFORCERS*.

SCIENTISTS DO NOT WORK IN A SOCIAL VACUUM. THEY'RE MOST PRODUCTIVE IN ENVIRONMENTS WHERE SCIENTIFIC ACTIVITY RECEIVES CONSIDERABLE SOCIAL AND/OR MATERIAL REINFORCEMENT. IN RECENT YEARS MANY BASIC RESEARCH PSYCHOLOGISTS HAVE GONE OUT OF THE LABORATORY TO WORK IN THE SCHOOLS AND HOSPITALS.

SAY, THAT'S REALLY GRATIFYING TO HEAR. IT'S A HEARTWARMING TREND— PEOPLE REACHING OUT TO HELP PEOPLE.

INTERESTINGLY ENOUGH, THOSE WHO ARE MOVING INTO THE APPLIED AREAS DO TALK QUITE A BIT ABOUT THE OVERALL BETTERMENT OF MANKIND. BUT IT'S IN THE APPLIED AREAS WHERE IT'S GENERALLY EASIEST TO FIND SOCIAL REINFORCEMENT, THE KIND OF THING YOU WERE DISHING OUT IN THE PREVIOUS BALLOON.

THE VALUE OF WORKING WITH A PIGEON IS LESS *OBVIOUS* THAN THE VALUE OF A *FRONTAL ATTACK* ON MENTAL ILLNESS.

IN MOST SITUATIONS THIS SORT OF DOWN-TO-EARTH WORK PROVIDES MORE PRAISE, APPROVAL AND GENERAL ATTENTION FROM OTHER PEOPLE, SO MANY PSYCHOLOGISTS FIND THEIR BEHAVIOR GOING WHERE THOSE SOCIAL REINFORCERS ARE FOUND.

HOWEVER, THERE ARE STILL SOME PLACES THAT DISH OUT MORE SOCIAL REINFORCEMENT FOR PURE SCIENTIFIC RESEARCH, AND SCIENTISTS WHO FIND THEMSELVES IN SUCH PLACES ARE USUALLY BEHAVING IN A MANNER THAT PRODUCES THOSE SOCIAL REINFORCERS.

YOU MUST KIND OF HATE TO ADMIT THIS TO YOURSELF.

TRUE. EVEN EXPERIMENTAL PSYCHOLOGISTS FIND IT AVERSIVE TO STATE THAT THEIR MOST NOBLE BEHAVIOR, THAT OF BEING A SCIENTIST, IS PRIMARILY UNDER THE CONTROL OF SOCIAL AND MATERIAL REINFORCERS OUTSIDE OF THE SCIENTIFIC REALM.

RECAP

This chapter illustrates how events that seem like natural or unconditioned reinforcers are really learned or conditioned reinforcers. Since we are almost always in contact with conditioned reinforcers, like attention and social approval, we tend to take it for granted that they are unconditioned reinforcers. The fact is that there are relatively few unconditioned reinforcers. Most of our behavior is maintained by conditioned reinforcers.

OBJECTIVES

1. When we talk about learning as its own reinforcement, we mean that it is _____.
   a) intrinsically reinforcing
   b) extrinsically reinforcing
   c) an unconditioned reinforcer
   d) a conditioned reinforcer
   e) a & c
   f) b & d

2. According to the text, it is likely that learning and truth are _____.
   a) conditioned reinforcers
   b) unconditioned reinforcers
   c) unconditioned aversive stimuli
   d) b & c

3. It is not likely that learning and truth are _____ (according to the text).
   a) primary reinforcers
   b) secondary reinforcers
   c) unconditioned reinforcers
   d) a & c
   e) b & c

4. Even scientists' research behaviors are primarily controlled by _____.
   a) intrinsic reinforcers
   b) extrinsic reinforcers
   c) social reinforcement
   d) a & c
   e) b & c

5. We behave in ways that help us acquire a maximum amount of _____.
   a) reinforcement
   b) extinction
   c) punishment
   d) behavior

6. When we behave in ways that help us acquire a maximum amount of reinforcement, we are exhibiting _____.
   a) discrimination behavior
   b) differentiation behavior
   c) respondent behavior
   d) a & c

ANSWERS
1. e; 2. a; 3. d; 4. e; 5. a; 6. a.

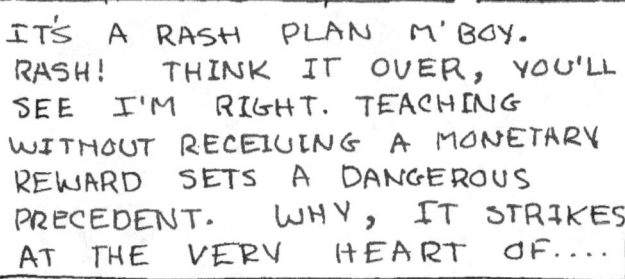

LEARNING IS REALLY A REINFORCER FOR NEARLY ALL STUDENTS.

DIG THIS, GUYS:
$\sigma x^2 = \frac{\Sigma F(X - ux^2)}{N} =$
$\frac{\Sigma F x^2}{N} =$
$\Sigma \left(\frac{F}{N}\right) x^2 =$
$\Sigma P x^2$

SHADDAP!

DROP DEAD!

TURN OUT THAT LIGHT! IT'S THREE IN THE MORNING!

AND LEARNING THAT IS USEFUL OR RELEVANT IN THE REAL WORLD IS THE MOST REINFORCING.....

SUDDENLY, THE MYTHIC MODIFIER'S TRAIN OF THOUGHT IS INTERRUPTED BY ANGRY CRIES AND THE SOUND OF SHATTERING GLASS.

WOT!

SAVE ME, BEHAVIOR WOMAN!

PROFESSOR! WHAT'S THE MATTER!

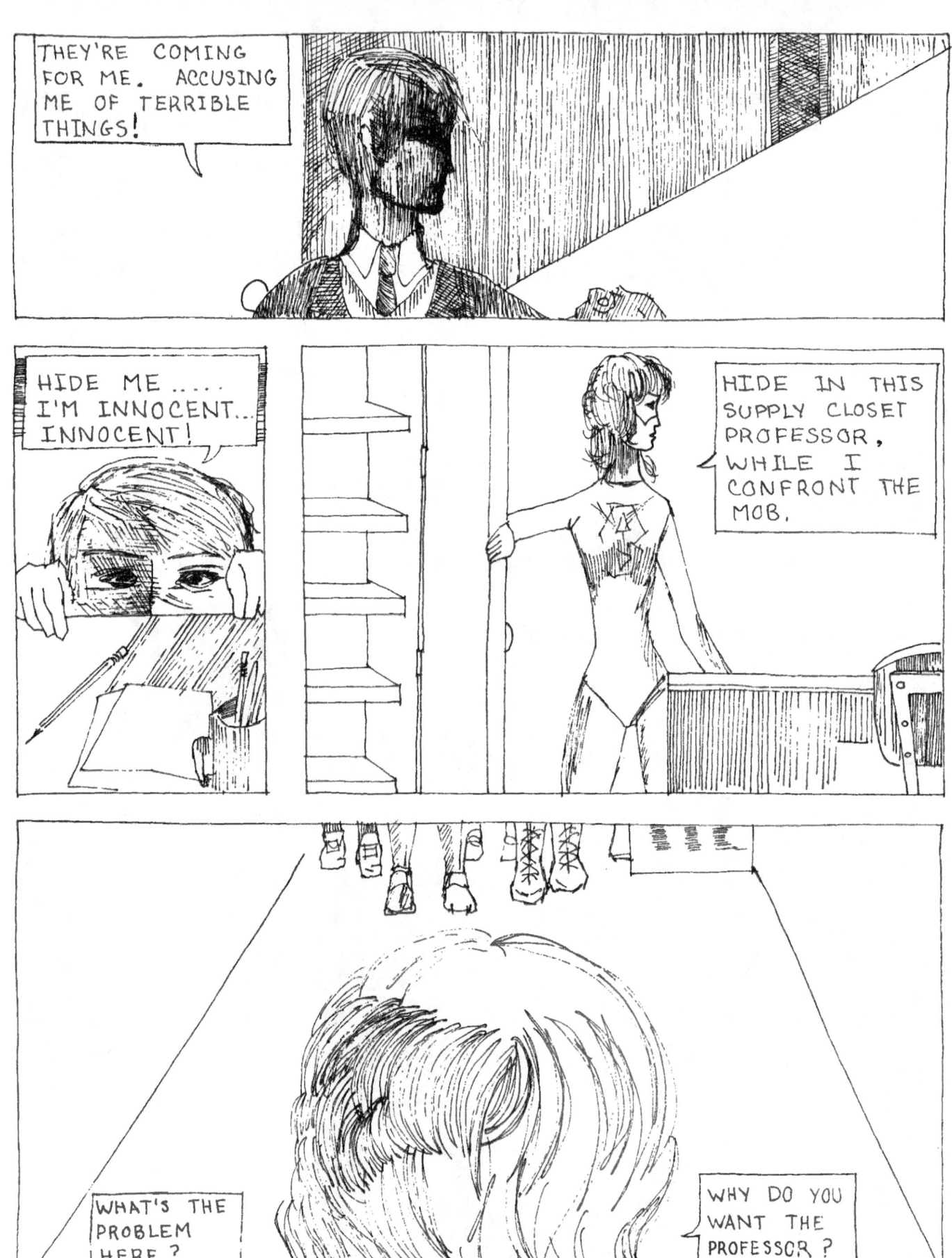

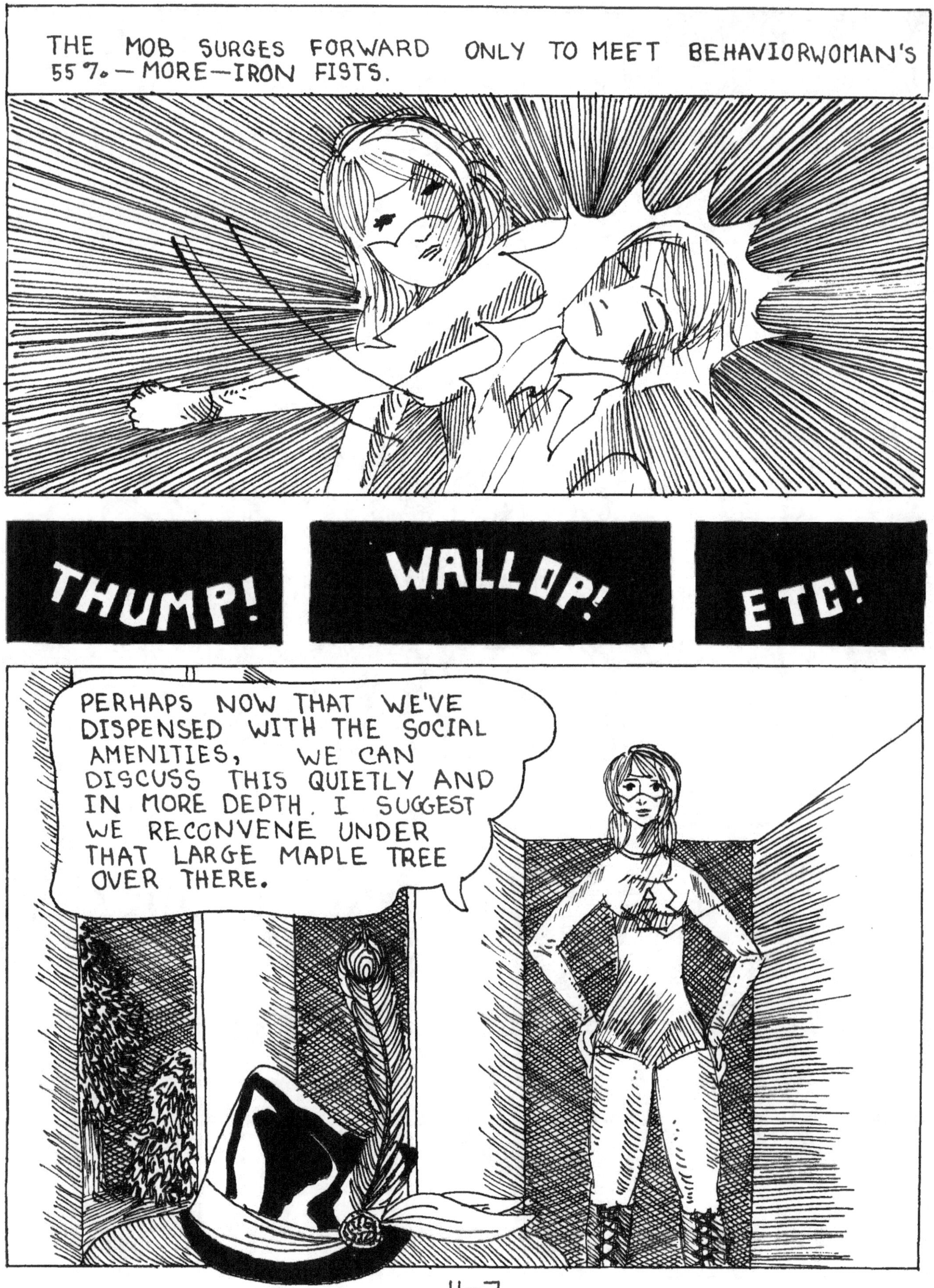

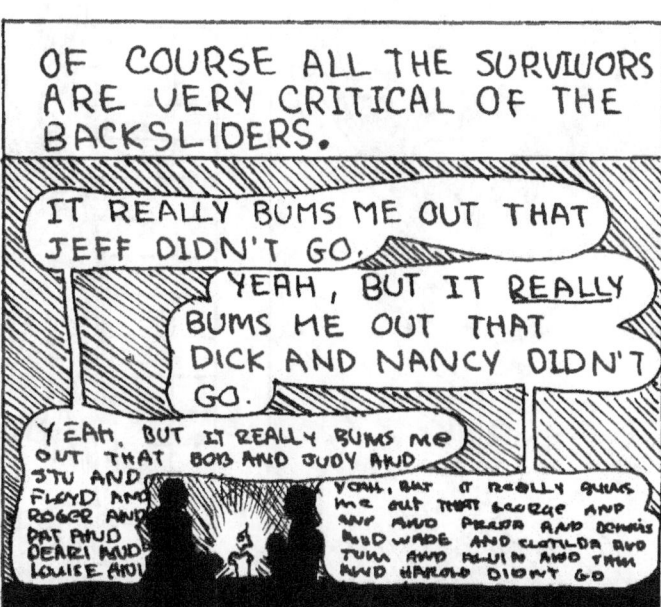

 RIGHT, AND BY THE END OF THE SEMESTER ONLY A HANDFUL OF STUDENTS ARE LEFT, AND BY THIS TIME, EVEN THE INSTRUCTOR MAY HAVE DISAPPEARED.

 MY PROJECT WAS AT THE CRITICAL STAGE WHEN OUR PROF QUIT.

 AFTER A YEAR OR TWO OF OPERATION, THE FREE UNIVERSITY CLOSES ITS DOORS BECAUSE OF LACK OF INTEREST ON THE PART OF STUDENTS AND FACULTY ALIKE.

 NOW WAIT A MINUTE, I CAN THINK OF AT LEAST TWO REASONS WHY THE FREE UNIVERSITIES WOULD FAIL.

FOR ONE THING, THE PRESENT SYSTEM CONTAMINATES MOST STUDENTS. PEOPLE WHO GROW UP EXPECTING ARTIFICIAL REWARDS — LIKE GRADES — WON'T BE ABLE TO MAKE IT OUTSIDE THE SYSTEM.

 HERE YA ARE KIDS: DOWNERS — YER D'S AND E'S; UPPERS — YER C'S AND B'S — AND WILD CRAZY A'S. ENOUGH A'S AND YOU'LL REALLY TRIP.... YOU'LL THINK YOU'RE IN LINE FOR THE SCEOND VICE PRESIDENCY OF THE MOXIE BOTTLING COMPANY AND A SPLIT LEVEL IN THE SUBURBS.. AND

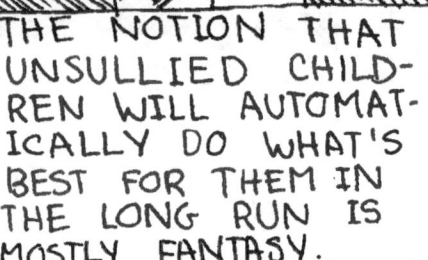

A STUDENT AT THE FREE UNIVERSITY HAS TOO MANY GOOD REASONS NOT TO STUDY OR ATTEND CLASS.
  IT'S TOO COLD AND RAINY.....

OR TOO HOT AND DRY.....

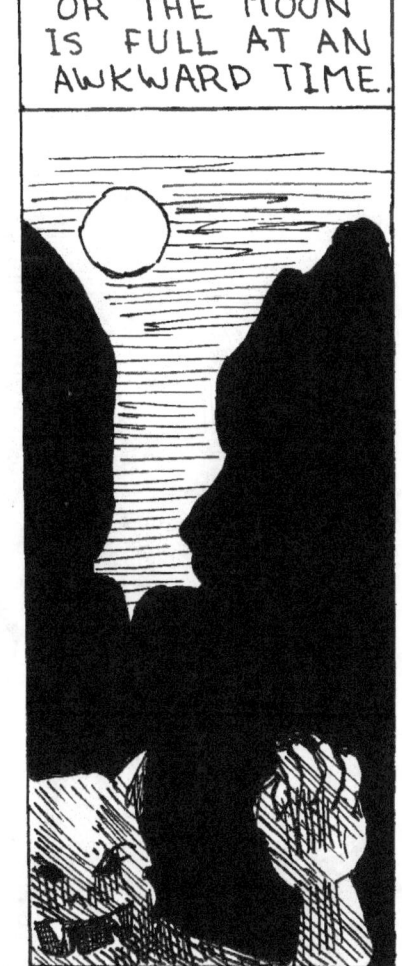

OR THE MOON IS FULL AT AN AWKWARD TIME.

OR A GOOD FRIEND DROPS IN. YOU HAVEN'T SEEN HIM IN A LONG TIME; IT WOULD BE RUDE AND ROTTEN TO GO TO YOUR ORGANIC GARDENING CLASS THAT NIGHT. YOU PLAN TO GO NEXT TIME.

YEAH, THE COAST IS REALLY......
.... GOT BUSTED, AND........
..... REALLY GREAT GRASS......
COUPLE HUNDRED FEET OF FILM ..... W.C. FIELDS.
HESSE REALLY

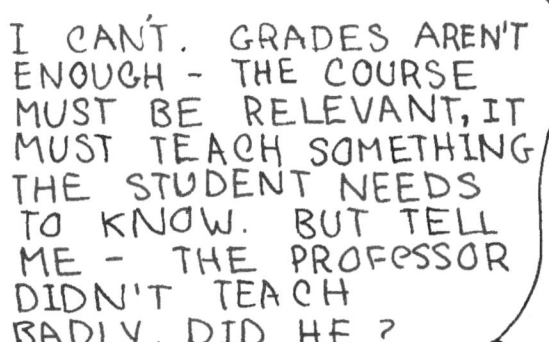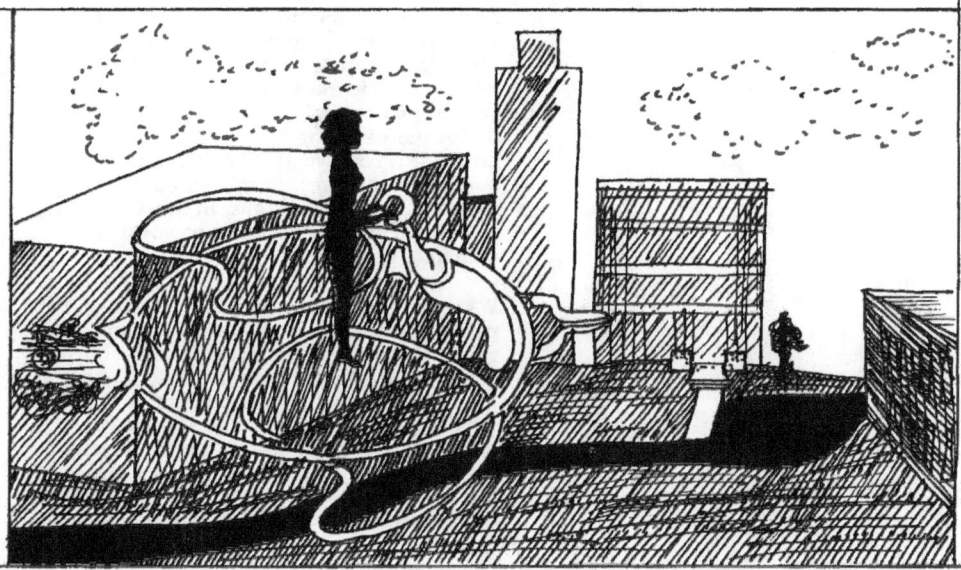

RECAP

1. Reinforcer effectiveness varies for different people. Just because a specific event is reinforcing for one person doesn't mean it will be reinforcing for everyone. It is for this very reason that educators cannot rely on the reinforcing capability of "learning" to control all student's behavior. For some students learning alone will be sufficient to maintain study behavior; however, most students require additional contingencies. Also, there will be some courses where even the best students don't find the subject matter reinforcing. The entire idea presented, concerning learning as a reinforcer, refers back to the difference between a reward and a reinforcer. Some people value "learning," and for them it might be a reinforcer. However, the final criterion for an event to be designated a reinforcer is that it increases the frequency of the behavior it follows. (A reward must only be appealing.) In this empirical look at "learning," it fails, in most cases, to be a sufficient reinforcer to control academic behavior.

2. We are not advocating that all attention be paid to grades and no attention given to the subject matter. The most effective contingency management system would be one that utilized as many reinforcers as possible. Grades can be effective; and interesting, relevant text material can also be effective. A system that utilizes both, grades and interesting material, can be more effective than a system that utilizes only one or the other.

OBJECTIVES

1. Learning CAN be its own reward.
   a. true
   b. false

2. Learning is always enough of a reward to maintain studying.
   a. true
   b. false

3. Learning is:
   a. a powerful reinforcer
   b. a weak reinforcer
   c. a powerful punisher
   d. a weak punisher
   e. b & d

4. Two reasons why free universities fail were presented. These reasons are:
   a. The present system contaminates students, so they expect grades.
   b. Free universities can't compete with the regular universities against this contamination because the regular university already has control.

5. In free experimental situations where "uncontaminated" students were used, students spent the least amount of time doing what?
   a. arts
   b. sports
   c. playing
   d. reading, writing, arithmetic
   e. crafts

6. The belief that grades, rules, and instructions have a debilitating effect, and that man will learn on his own if left alone (learning is its own reward), is
   a. supported empirically.
   b. the most parsimonious assumption.
   c. just a philosophy, lacking data.
   d. backed by several experiments.
   e. the accepted goal of our present educational system.

ANSWERS

1. a; 2. b; 3. b; 5. d; 6. c.

TABLE OF CONTENTS

- CAPTAIN CON. MAN 1-1
- Y'ARE WHAT 'CHA DO 2-1
- BEHAVIORMAN I 3-1
- BEHAVIORMAN II 4-1
- SUMMARY I 5-1
- SUMMARY II 6-1
- BEHAVIORWOMAN I 7-1
- BEHAVIORWOMAN II 8-1
- FIRST FLY-BY NIGHT, UNDERGROUND EXPERIMENTAL COLLEGE .. 9-1
- DOCTOR NICE 10-1
- BEHAVIORWOMAN III 11-1

THE FOLLOWING SCHOLARS ARE PRIMARILY LIABLE FOR PERPETRATING THIS TEXT ON THE UNSUSPECTING PUBLIC.

WRITING — RICHARD W. MALOTT, PH.D.

ART + GHOST WRITING — PAT HARTLEP, B.A.

ART — STUART HARTLEP, A.A.

CALIGRAPHY — PATIENCE VAUGHN, B.F.A.

PHOTOGRAPHY — JAMES E. SMITH, BPA

COPY EDITING — ROBERT LUDLOW, M.A.

EDUCATIONAL TECHNOLOGY — DAN REESE

EDUCATIONAL TECHNOLOGY — DICK WOLFENDEN

BEHAVIORDELIA, P.O. BOX 1044,
KALAMAZOO, MICH. 49001
PHONE - 382-5611

www.ingramcontent.com/pod-product-compliance
Lightning Source LLC
Chambersburg PA
CBHW080728230426
43665CB00020B/2666